PRAISE FOR RETURNING TO REAL

This book, *Returning to Real, Embracing the We in Me, A Wounds to Wellness Guidebook* is a perfect package! Two skilled psychotherapists in print are always there...in your purse, on your phone or tablet, ready to support and guide you. Suzanne Rochon and Carmen Jelly Weiss have creatively combined their years of experience and genuine compassion to bring clarity, optimism and relief to the most common personality traits that develop as a result of our (mis)-interpretation of life events. Their experiential stories and belief in Raw, Risky, and Real, support each concept and encourage the reader to take action and make progress on their life journey; one brave step and one encouraging word at a time. A must-read and a gift to treasure.

Suzanne Harmony
International Best-Selling Author
HarmonyHelps.ca

Like sitting down with a trusted friend who embraces you and your scars unconditionally, *Returning to Real* is one of those rare books that you will return to again and again for advice and guidance as you navigate life's waters. I already have a list of people to whom I'll gift this gem because I know it will be a life-changing companion.

Gina Clark
Artist, Creativity Mentor

Wow!! I have read this book slowly over the last few weeks and I feel as though I have been on a very reflective journey...one that I have thoroughly enjoyed! Bravo, you two! I think you have written a wonderfully comprehensive book that provides a nice balance between content and exercises. The inclusion of the real stories and vignettes are useful to illustrate many of the points that you are describing. This book is easy to read. You have presented a very welcoming and conversational style of writing and it's almost as if I am sitting in the room with you and we are having a chat. I would highly recommend this book to anyone. I think that this would be a book that you could return to time and time again as we continue on our life's journey.

Tina Benevedis, PhD

First of all, I loved this book. It taught me a lot about myself and also helped teach me things I can bring to my own clients.

Jenny-Lee Brunet, BSW, RSW

To get the best experience from this guidebook, listen to our podcasts to access another way of anchoring and integrating the material and to take the next steps needed to Return to Real.

RETURNING TO REAL • A podcast on Anchor

Visit our websites:

Suzanne: www.imaginelifesolutions.ca

Carmen: www.newperceptions.ca

DEDICATION

This book is dedicated to all souls who are feeling the hunger to embody their truth and to fully express their power and potential. As we heal our wounds, we clear the way for our authentic power to manifest in the world.

Our deepest and most sincere gratitude goes to our publisher, As You Wish Publishing. Thank you to Todd and Kyra for your belief in our work and your efforts to bring this book into being. Your wisdom, guidance, expertise, and friendship has meant so much to us. Indeed, this book would not be published without your confidence and belief in our vision.

We would also like to thank our clients, students, listeners, and readers... You are the focus!

Carmen

Thank you to my husband, Tony, for being a great partner and for supporting me in my journey down many paths. Thank you for encouraging me to direct my strong will in a way that helps me develop it as a gift in my life and in the lives of those around me. Words cannot express my gratitude for your steady and unwavering support.

Thank you to my parents, Lorne and Bev, who did the best they knew how with very little insight on how to raise a go-get-'em stubborn daughter like me. Thanks for teaching me about perseverance, good work ethic and fighting for what I believe in.

Thank you to my three daughters, Taylor, Loren, and Sydney who show me every day what it is to live our truth simply and clearly. You have been three of my greatest teachers. Thank you to my grandchildren Milo, Emry and Lenora who motivate me to live strong and healthy.

And finally, a wholehearted thank you to my remarkable clients who gave time and emotional energy to share personal stories, so that other people could be helped. This book could not have been written without your vulnerability, courage, and strength.

Suzanne

I am eternally grateful to those who taught me there are other ways of being and other paths to follow than those I imagined for myself.

Carmen and Fern (aka Mom and Dad) your continued commitment to life as a couple has taught me about love, support, resilience, and courage.

Ron, to the world you have a developmental disability, to me you have the greatest superpower of all- you are real. You laugh when it is funny, you stomp off when you are angry and you cry when you are sad. You teach me about unconditional love and that connection is the most important thing we have.

Max, Alex, and Jonah, you have been my beacon of light through dark times. From you, I continue to learn and practice acceptance, patience, compassion, kindness and to let go. You stayed the course and believed I could be a better parent. Thank you.

Joel, I could not have imagined on that full moon September evening when our paths crossed some 23 years ago that life would be what it is today! BEing with you is magical.

Table of Contents

AUTHOR'S NOTE	XIII
OUR INTENTION	XV
1. Raw, Risky & Real™	1
2. The Inner Critic Part in Me	21
3. The People Pleaser Part in Me	41
4. The Perfectionist and the Expert Parts of Me	61
5. The Imposter Part in Me	83
6. The Rescuer Part in Me	99
7. The Victim Part in Me	113
8. Returning to Real Acceptance of the We in Me	131
ABOUT THE AUTHORS	143
REFERENCES	147

AUTHOR'S NOTE

Together, we would like to acknowledge the impact of Dr. Gabor Maté's Compassionate Inquiry approach. As graduates of the year long course and of the mentorship program we recognize how deeply transformative our time in the CI community was and continues to be. The impetus for putting pen to paper was the self-reflective journey of CI and for this we are deeply grateful.

This book is written from our hearts, blending research from (but not limited to) Cognitive Behavioural Therapy, Dialectical Behaviour Therapy, Compassionate Inquiry, Internal Family Systems, Acceptance and Commitment Therapy, Positive Psychology, Feminine Theory, Attachment Research, Neuroscience, Systems Theory, and Spirituality as well as a myriad of relational and somatic philosophies, and our own personal stories. This book is a product of decades of research and ours and our clients' personal healing journeys.

The nature of perception is subjective and rooted in the observer's own experience. The personal and client examples in this book are based on our perceptions of people and events that took place in our childhood and across our lifespan. We have done our best to be accurate when describing recollections of people and situations. We want to be clear that these perspectives are not statements of fact but of our own personal perceptions.

Apart from the authors' names, Carmen and Suzanne, all other names attached to personal stories are fictitious in order to protect the confidentiality and privacy of individuals.

OUR INTENTION

Life is hard. Every day, people struggle with big and small decisions, relationships, grief, addictions, trauma, change and choice points.

This book is meant to be a guide for people of all ages, regardless of identity. As you read through the pages, you will find stories of real people. The stories' purpose is to illustrate specific examples and to provide real-life experiences you may identify with or learn from. You may experience discomfort, resistance or other unsettling thoughts and feelings. These triggers are normal.

We recognize how difficult life is and that the strategies we utilize to cope are often temporary. Self care in the way we understand it in our society may not create lasting results. You will notice we have moved away from using the term self-care in this book, as it is wildly over-used and often misunderstood. Self-care as we predominantly understand it in our distraction-driven, FOMO (fear of missing out) culture is an external activity that is meant to make us feel better. When we hear the words self-care, we think of taking a bath, getting a massage or a facial, taking a walk, going to the gym, doing yoga and more. While these are all valuable and we should make room in our lives for these types of activities as a form of relaxation and care for ourselves, we wonder what happens when you do all these things and still don't feel better. Have you noticed that some of these self-care activities we engage in are typically in response to stress? Is this familiar?

"I really should book a massage. My neck and shoulders are so tight. I am under a lot of stress at work."

"It's Friday night, and it's been a long and stressful week. Let me run myself a bath and pour a glass of wine for some relaxation."

Or are you a retreat junkie? Here is an example from Suzanne's life. For years, I attended retreats and workshops searching for the answer to all my problems, believing the retreat was good self-care. While the time away and the learning was wonderful and invaluable, I did, time and again, return on Sunday evening to the same issues I had left with on Friday night. I thought I had left the problems at home on my way to the retreat only to realize many, many years later that the problem had tagged along. I finally realized that both the problem and the source of the solution were deeply held within me, and while a retreat or a massage were helpful and made me feel better in the moment, a consistent practice of inquiry using the Raw, Risky & Real™ was a key component to reclaiming my authentic self.

We could keep going, but you get the message that we employ these self-care strategies in response to stress. Please keep taking care of yourself and attending retreats and workshops; they are important, but let's also help you explore other, perhaps more sustainable strategies.

We are interested in helping you deepen your experience and in offering you practices that begin to shift your awareness and tap into those core aspects of yourself that shape your life.

We wrote this book with the intention to help you become the best version of yourself through awareness of the various parts of yourself. Throughout the book we may refer to these parts as the We in Me. The pages of the book offer you the opportunity to see these triggers as gifts.

The goal of this book is to help you return to real. This is someone who lives authentically and is connected and attuned to their body, mind, and spirit. As a result, you may develop a unique approach to life that honours and supports your authenticity and eliminates the need for subpersonalities to take over.

For more than twenty-five years, we have worked in the field of psychotherapy, social work, supervision, mental health, and personal and professional transformation. For decades we have assisted people in re-discovering their real selves. We have found that it does not take "capital T" trauma or abuse to wound a person. All it takes is not seeing them for who they really are and parenting or relating in a way that does not honour a child's true nature. This is nobody's fault as most of us are raised by people who do not ultimately understand their true nature. We are trained to "be" someone we are not. Deep inside, we believe we are not good enough, giving way to the creation of subpersonalities which are intended to protect us from the pain of not being seen for who we are. You are not inherently flawed. You have learned how to adapt and survive.

Many of today's adaptive strategies provide us with quick fixes. These kinds of solutions are reactionary and conditional, and they simply do not provide long-term results. They focus on reacting and controlling behaviours rather than understanding and honouring the root cause.

We believe you were drawn to this book for a reason. Perhaps, deep down you have a desire to be fully expressive and committed to living true to your nature. This is great as you are no longer willing to remain in your woundedness.

By applying the practices in this guidebook, we imagine you honouring who you truly are. We hope you will experience more harmony in your relationship with self and others. This book will provide you with insight and tools needed to support you in living real to your nature.

This book is written from the perspective of therapists as wounded healers, who, as human beings first and foremost, have experienced personal trauma, pain, and suffering. We recognize that irrespective of our gender identity, skin colour, age, religion, social status, or career choice, we all struggle with the nature of the mind. Our stories are no different than the average person's childhood experience of loving, well-intended parents carrying their own wounds and trying to do the best they could. That's code for having experienced or been witness to the spectrum of human experiences of trauma, loss, addictions, anxiety, depression, separation, divorce, self-doubt, guilt, shame and so much more. While often unconscious, it is not uncommon for therapists or those in the helping profession to choose their career path as a result of what they have experienced. It is through the pain of these experiences that we ourselves were propelled to follow a path of healing, growth, and discovery.

The journey through our own dark nights of the soul, or those we have had the honour of witnessing and holding space for, enabled us to recognize our own return to real and the calling to share our insights and stories with you in this guidebook.

Nothing in these pages is necessarily original, but it is unique to us. We have been deeply inspired by many fellow therapists, social workers, light workers, philosophers, academics, spiritual teachers, and our clients. We have drawn from those who have come before us to assist those who are with us to pave the way for those yet to come.

This book is experiential and is intended as a guide for returning to the authentic self in which we were born. This authentic self is the part of us that is invisible yet ever present and patient. It merely waits at the ready, to emerge as we make way for it through awareness, healing, and self- development.

We invite you, from a place of love, to take our hand and walk this journey with us.

Chapter 1

Raw, Risky & Real™

"Lean into your fears. Go to your outer edges. Because the place where your greatest limit lives is also the place where your greatest growth lies." Robin Sharma

THERE IS ALWAYS A Beginning. Giving birth is a painful process. Those reading this who have birthed a child may be reminded of the excruciating waves of pain lasting longer than one can even imagine possible to endure. While intense pain during the birthing process is not every woman's story, it is for the majority. Those who supported their partners throughout the bearing of creation may also be transported back to that moment, as you read this. For most of us remembering a painful birth, whether as an active participant or as a witness, our attention may also immediately turn to the beautiful and precious outcome of that birth.

The manifestation of the *Raw, Risky & Real™* framework, which is the foundation of this book, is the story of a birth, of sorts.

The Raw, Risky & Real™ Framework

Raw, Risky & Real™ is an intuitive model to describe the process of returning to real. This model is a supportive tool to help you understand the truth of who you really are. Our personality describes our behaviour, but it doesn't explain it. We adapt our personalities to the expectations of others. We often receive messages or are parented in a way that encourages us to develop a personality at odds with our real nature. Think about your own childhood. There were probably rules or expectations that forced you to feel insecure, fit in or to survive. There are no tests to take; this model is designed to be intuitive, personal, and empowering. It's time to discover your unique self. Your journey into this book starts with your own answer to this question:

Who am I and who do I want to be?

What is your reason for wanting to heal? The answer to this question really matters. An example may be to heal your wounds to become a better grandparent than the parent you were to your children. You might want to release the anxiety or sadness that you carry. Perhaps you feel lost, confused, unsettled or overwhelmed. You might be looking for healthier coping strategies or perhaps your motivation for healing your wounds is simply to explore other aspects of yourself. Understanding your own unique reasons for wanting to change and grow helps create the space for you to embrace and express your vulnerability (raw emotions); to stand your ground, speak your truth and move into action (risky); and to shine from your internal reference point, your authentic self (real).

So how do we heal our childhood experiences and move from wounds to wellness?

We developed the Raw, *Risky & Real*™ framework as a way of interpreting and integrating your experiences. *Raw, Risky & Real*™ considers body, mind, and spirit qualities. Returning to real is our philosophy for healing our wounds based on the model of getting to know our subpersonalities.

Buddha states that to be human is painful, but suffering is optional. Sometimes things happen to us that we did not expect – the loss of a relationship we thought would last forever, the end of a job or career, a sudden symptom in the body, an unexpected depression or loss of meaning. There are also the current broader world issues, the confusion of social structures, questionable government practices, economic instability, unsustainable healthcare systems, and perhaps most importantly the destruction of the earth. We seem to be carrying the weight of the world right now which is why it is crucial to understand our emotions, thoughts and behaviours as a way of healing.

"Emotions are currents of energy that pass through us. Awareness of these currents is the first step in learning how our experiences come into learning and why."

Gary Zukav- The Seat of the Soul

We must feel our raw wounds, pain, and discomfort in order to grow and change. The stimulus for change is feeling and leaning into the discomfort and pain. This is counterintuitive because we have been taught to move away from pain. In order to survive, we have learned many strategies to distract, avoid and numb our difficult experiences and emotions. The tendency to protect ourselves creates our unique subpersonalities. Our inner worlds can be viewed as different subpersonalities that hold emotions, perceptions, and belief systems. This is what we refer to as the We in Me.

Raw Risky & Real™ is a mindful approach that will help you recognize raw spots and discover which of the subpersonalities you default to when you need to escape the pain of your wounds, experience high-pressure situations, or feel highly stressed. Using this framework is a bit like healing a wound from the inside out. It is not about putting a bandage on a bullet hole. We go deep inside to the source of pain and heal by moving outward. We must mindfully connect to the wound and/or symptoms that we hold in our bodies. They often manifest as tension, tightness, tingling or any body-felt sensation. These sensations may seem foreign and unfamiliar to you as we often disconnect in order to survive and move forward.

In the worst case scenario, we are numb and not connected to what's happening in our bodies. You may be seen as distant, cold, and unapproachable. You may be suspicious of people's motives, have trouble connecting in relationships with others, and sometimes fake what you're supposed to feel and how you are supposed to act in certain situations. Perhaps you feel lost and disconnected. The intent of the *Raw Risky & Real*™ framework is to re-connect you to your body, all your subpersonalities and your real self. *This is your return to real!*

Most of us live in a highly externally referenced world. We look to this outside world to create our identities. We look to others for validation, affirmation, and to make meaning. We are unaware how much of our life is determined by how someone else responds (or doesn't respond) to us. This is because we need attachment for survival. When we must make a choice between our attachment and authenticity needs, attachment always wins. The good news is that we can have both. It is truly life changing to reclaim our authenticity, experiences, sensations, and choices, and begin to move forward with trust and commitment in our internal world.

A Peek at Subpersonalities - the parts of us that make up the We in Me

We are all born with our authenticity intact and with love as our primary emotion, yet all humans develop subpersonalities. In simple terms, a subpersonality is a pattern of behaviour that has evolved over time as a protective mechanism whose primary purpose is to protect us from pain and suffering. You might recognize these subpersonalities as the incessant little voices in your head telling you how bad, incompetent, not important, or overly important you are; that people don't like you; that you are lazy and more. Within us, there are many different parts, like how an orchestra has a variety of musicians. We are each an orchestra with many instruments competing for a solo. In other words, the natural state of the human mind is multiplicity.

It helps to be aware that different people experience their parts differently; there is no right way. Recognizing and understanding our subpersonalities is concerned with what works, not what's right. The idea is to be able to find, within yourself, something you can repeatedly identify. People have experienced their parts as images, voices, sounds or physical sensations.

Let us give you an example from Carmen's life. When training for a race, I will set my alarm clock for 5 am to get up and exercise. However, when my alarm sings with the birds, another part of me wonders, "What the heck! Do I really need to do this?" This is the voice of my inner critic, an inner protector inside me. For most people, that inner critic is often grumbling away, looking for something to find fault with. It shines a light on small failings and shifts them into big ones, repeatedly punishing you for things long past. For example, "Why bother training if you aren't fast or young and you will only injure yourself again?"

My inner critic is trying to protect me from failing. Once I recognize my inner critic and appreciate that she is trying to protect me, I can compassionately realize her purpose rather than assuming she is speaking the truth. Believing the internal dialogue initiates the shame storm. The only healthy purpose of guilt or shame is for learning, not punishment! Anything beyond the point of learning is needless suffering. We do not need to believe what we think.

The inner critic is just a subpersonality. Because we have many subpersonalities that are trying to protect us, we slowly become alienated from our authenticity through the development of perceptions and behaviours known as personality. Our authenticity is tucked away and lost to our many parts. The journey back to our authentic self requires a courageous heart. The courage to heal is an ongoing journey whereby we come to know our parts while moving bravely forward into the future.

While there are several subpersonalities, in this book we will explore in more detail only those we have either experienced personally or have met more frequently in sessions with clients. The following image is a visual representation of our subpersonalities (We) overtaking our authentic self (Me). Notice how small the real you is in relation to the other parts of you.

In many therapies, and in some of the early thinking in the field of psychology, the way to deal with these parts of ourselves was rather harsh with an attempt to get rid of them. In this guidebook, you will only see compassionate curiosity as we lead you through the world that created these personalities and the space in which we can begin to befriend and integrate them.

What happened to our authenticity? Why do we have so many wounded adults in the world?

Some people experience capital "T" trauma, such as neglect, physical, emotional, or sexual abuse, or climate disaster, war and unexpected catastrophes. There is also small "t" trauma that often goes unrecognized. Some environments are unable to provide the safety we need to thrive and flourish. For example, some approaches to parenting are wounding parenting styles, meaning they are unintentionally wounding children. They are not meant to be hurtful. In fact, any given parenting style may work for certain children and not for others. Standard parenting styles do not always consider a child's true nature.

The easiest way to wound a child is to not embrace their true self, thus ignoring, judging or squashing that nature. The truth is our true self will keep nudging us until we find our way back. In the meantime, we disconnect from our authenticity and let our subpersonalities take the lead roles in our lives.

How do we discover our subpersonalities and shift from having them drive our bus rather than our own true nature being in the driver's seat?

Let's begin.

RAW is about feeling our pain points. We all have painful raw wounds simply because we are humans living life. That is the human experience. RAW is the beginning and the birthplace of change.

R: RECOGNIZE all modes of information moving through you in body, mind, and spirit. Notice your thoughts, feelings, and body sensations. Do you feel expansive, alert, and expressive or tight, constricted, or short of breath? Bring awareness to the experience in your body. By acknowledging all that is present, we give ourselves permission to get curious. Focus on a particular space in your body that is calling for your attention. Stay with the sensation for as long as you can. As you stay with the sensation, think of a word that reflects the sensation. If it could speak, what would it say? What does it need or want? Is there an emotion under this sensation?

A: ACKNOWLEDGE any discomfort or anything that is present in your body. Discomfort is a sign that you are triggered and that your past is showing up in your present. This is how you know a part has been activated.

W: WELCOME with compassion all that is present. This is the beginning of uncovering your parts, your subpersonalities.

To recap what you just read:

RECOGNIZE fully

ACKNOWLEDGE triggers

WELCOME parts

Subpersonalities have pure, honest intentions of protecting you from further pain and harm. As you get to know all parts of yourself, you will transform your relationship with difficult thoughts, feelings, and beliefs. We are creatures of habit, but we can change the way we dance with our subpersonalities by changing the music.

RISKY is about taking action.

"Courage is not the absence of fear, but fear walking." Susan David

Let's face it, it is risky to open up. This is where vulnerability dances with our adaptive strategies. We may fail, and that's OK. This is a journey and a circle that we will keep looping through.

This step is an incredible place for growth and change. This is where we will take action and engage in new practices. Creating new practices leads to manifesting new relationships with our subpersonalities and our real self.

Risky is an opportunity to reflect on your values and intentions so that you can write a new story. The story starts with being kind to ourselves and finding a balance that works for us.

R: REFLECTION: Reflecting on our values allows us to uncover what is meaningful and important to us from the perspective of our heart. Our values are the basic beliefs that determine our priorities and actions and they shape how we live, work and love. They measure whether or not our life is turning out the way we want to live. When our goals and choices align with our values, life is good. When our choices and goals do not align, we probably feel unhappy, stressed, or discontented with life. Your reflections provide clarity, direction, and motivate you to make important changes.

I: INTENTIONS: We provide ourselves accountability through intention setting, allowing us to take control of our choices and life. It's about being proactive in your own life, by purposely choosing how you want your life experience to be. Intentions prepare us for a moment in the future.

S: STORY: With intentions, we can write a new story for ourselves, filling the pages of the next chapter in our life. To truly change, we must first imagine what we want to create. Anything we can sense, feel, think about, observe, imagine can be manifested.

K: KINDNESS: Staring down our demons does not work. The push and pull of our parts' perceptions may attempt to sabotage our ability to write our new stories - our real life. We welcome each part with compassion and kindness.

Y: YEARNING: For any change to occur and to move us to the point of action we must want the change to occur. There must be a desire for something different.

To recap what you just read:

REFLECT on your values

Set INTENTIONS for what you want

Create the STORY of your life

Be KIND to all parts of yourself in the process

YEARN for what is possible

"You don't have to be great to start, but you have to start to be great." Zig Ziglar

REAL

We experience REAL as Brené Brown defines grounded confidence which is *"the messy process of learning and unlearning, practicing and failing, and surviving misses."*

Let's be clear, we don't arrive at REAL, we continually practice it, learning and unlearning, failing and succeeding, surviving and thriving.

R: REALIZATION: That REAL part of you has and will always be with you. This isn't about finding or creating your authentic self because that part of you, let's call it your soul, is not lost or needing to be created. We speak of it as a return because it is the place we come from. It has simply been covered up by our coping mechanisms and subpersonalities. It gently and patiently awaits your return.

E: EXPANSION: We are continually growing, changing, and expanding. Returning to our deepest, truest selves involves a continuous expansion of self, shifting from a rigid mindset to a more flexible mindset which supports new ideas and thoughts about ourselves and our world.

A: ACCEPTANCE: Acceptance is the greatest pathway out of suffering. Acceptance does not mean we agree with the circumstances of our life, it does not mean we simply roll over and let what is occurring continue to happen. It means that we acknowledge that in this moment, this is our reality.

L: LOVE: Love is transcendental. It is formless. At our very core, we are pure love. Before we can see others through the eyes of love, we must first see ourselves in this light.

To recap what you just read:

REALIZE that your authentic self has always been with you

EXPAND in new ways

ACCEPT your reality

LOVE yourself

"Sometimes being real means allowing pain or accepting a painful truth. Yet something in us aligns with an inner ground of authenticity when we are real. We love it because of its inherent rightness in our soul, the sense of 'Aha, here I am, and there is nothing to do but be." A. H Almaas

REALignment Practices

As you begin to immerse yourself in this book, we would like to offer you some daily REALignment practices to assist you in shifting out of your auto-pilot responses to more mindful and flexible responses, which you may find creates less stress and more balance in your life. Each chapter will offer a practice for mind, body, and spirit.

Not all practices in the book will resonate with you, and while we invite you to gravitate towards those that do speak to you, we suggest you try them all as a means of expanding yourself outside your comfort zone. Often, we find that those practices that initially feel awkward or unpleasant are the ones that bring much learning, growth, and insight.

Let's begin with the Raw, Risky & Real™ practice. We invite you to return to this practice as often as you can, want or need.

_____
_____
_____
_____
_____
_____
_____
_____
_____
_____
_____
_____
_____

REALign Your Mind Practice

The Raw, Risky & Real™ practice was created to assist you in moving through difficult and challenging aspects of your life. Always begin the practice by noticing your breath. You can close your eyes if that facilitates a connection, or you can hold a soft gaze. Notice the breath, without judgement, as it enters and leaves your body. Stay with the breath for at least three cycles.

RAW: Bring to mind a situation in your life that is uncomfortable, that you are dissatisfied with or that you would like to change. Begin to recognize your thoughts, feelings, and bodily sensations. Notice bodily sensations and allow feelings and emotions to emerge. Continue to notice what comes up, and welcome what may arise. This is the space in which we begin to connect with what is emerging. Stay with the sensations as long as is comfortable for you or for as long as you are willing to sit with the discomfort. Place your attention anywhere you feel pain, pressure, tension, and constriction and simply notice. This may seem unnatural to you as we are hardwired to move away from pain. For now, we invite you to simply notice.

Record anything that may have arisen. What do you notice in your body? What are your thoughts? What are you feeling, without judgement? Welcome anything that arises, without judgement.

_____
_____
_____
_____
_____
_____
_____
_____
_____
_____
_____
_____
_____

RISKY: This is where you begin to contemplate actions, hence the word risky, as sometimes moving to action may feel like a risk to our internal protective parts.

Here are prompts to guide you:

Reflect on your triggers and the messy parts of your life. What do you want to learn or unlearn? What is most important in your heart? What is significant and meaningful to you? Your reflections provide clarity and inspiration to take risks.

Intentions- Now that you have reflected on your triggers, you can begin imagining new ways of responding. What do you intend for yourself?

Story – With new intentions, what does your new story look like? What are the emotions that arise as you envision a different story for yourself?

Kindness- Are there areas in your life where you are not kind to yourself? Do you notice times when you are very critical and hard on yourself?

Yearn- What do you yearn for? What is out of balance in your life?

Record anything that emerges, remembering there is no right or wrong answer. Return to the breath and thank your internal wisdom, which is always with you. Take a moment to honour those parts of you that emerged.

Do you notice a colour? Is an image forming? Is a scent or sound surfacing for you? Are you guided to move your body? If so, go ahead and welcome the guidance to flow with your internal rhythm. Are you moved to write or to create? If so, here is some space.

REAL: Now is the time to begin exploring your authentic self. What does REAL mean to you? It's okay if nothing comes up right now. Remember this is a process. We encourage you to remember that your real self is within you and while it may be buried by some of the subpersonalities we will be exploring in the book, it is through reflecting on moments of curiosity, creativity, compassion or connection that allows us to imagine the possibilities.

We invite you to recall times when you experienced curiosity, creativity, compassion or connection. What were you doing? Who were you with? What was the experience like? How old were you?

It's okay if no explicit memories come to mind. Use the space below to draw anything that emerges, including what you imagine the future to look like. To complete the exercise, close your eyes and breathe deeply in and out for one minute and thank your internal wisdom.

REALign Your Body Practice

"Life is an act of letting go. You breathe in, breathe out. You can't hold on to anything."

Gurudev Sri Sri Ravi Shankar

These practices will support you in letting go of the overload and/or overwhelm you are carrying in your body. It is important to give yourself permission to come into an alignment with your own energy and body sensations. The goal is to feel the sensations and to allow them to be present. Where there is tension, bring attention. The result will be a state of relaxation and calm.

Body tension is often an energy imbalance. Prolonged periods of body stress and tension can lead to a myriad of mental and physical issues. We often can't think straight, or perhaps we shut down mentally, emotionally and physically. Sometimes we experience a sense of not being able to move forward and a lack of motivation and productivity.

This practice is an opportunity to pause and connect with your body. It works when you implement it with consistency. According to Robin Sharma in his book entitled *The 5AM Club*, he indicates it takes 66 days of consistent practice before you see massive and permanent shifts. Fortunately, this exercise is easy to perform. You can also do this exercise mentally if you aren't able to perform it physically.

The following grounding practice will bring you into your body.

If possible, do this exercise outside, barefoot on the grass or earth. If that is not possible, imagine you are outdoors or stream a nature video. Your energy will also respond to imagination, as energy follows thoughts. For obvious reasons, we suggest reviewing the steps before attempting the exercise or voice-record the steps on your phone for use at any time.

1. Stand up tall and straight and feel your feet connected to the earth. Take a few deep breaths and notice where you feel tension. Is it in your head, neck, shoulders, back, stomach, or any other body part?

2. Allow the sensation to be present without judgement. Just notice and breathe deeply into the area. Send loving kindness to the area with your thoughts. Perhaps you can send a ray of bright white light (or your favourite colour) from your heart to the areas that are holding tension. Imagine beams of light warming and soothing the area(s).

3. Sense the light surrounding the area. For the next 1 or 2 minutes, be with the sensation, thoughts, and emotions. Perhaps ask the tension, "If you could speak, what would you say?" Stay here as long as you feel comfortable.

4. If you received a message, thank the tension for its wisdom. If not, that's OK too.

5. With loving kindness, inform the tension that it is OK to soften and release.

6. Bend your knees so that you are sitting in a chair position. Raise your arms upward above your head and inhale deeply.

7. As you exhale, quickly push your arms straight down, as you stand up with your legs and feet. You are now standing in a tall tree position again.

8. Repeat this pattern as you alternate the chair pose (inhale) and tree pose (exhale) 3 to 6 more times.

9. As you stand up for the final time, wipe the tension from your body. Gently release with kindness as you wipe your body with your hands.

10. Sense your feet rooted strongly in the earth. Imagine the energy of peace coming up from the earth, into your feet, and through your entire body. Allow it to flow everywhere and all the way up to the top of your head. The earth's energy completely surrounds you. Breathe in the peace, receive it in your body and allow it to be. Breathe in. Breathe out. You are safe, and you are calm.

This exercise is not a *one and done* miracle. Keep doing it. When you feel tension, apply RAW, *relate* to the tension by *allowing* and *welcoming* it. This is an exercise to reset and refocus. With consistency over extended periods of time, it will become a habit.

"The truth about our childhood is stored up in our body, and although we repress it, we can never alter it. Our intellect can be deceived, our feelings manipulated, our perception confused, and our body tricked with medication. But someday the body will present its bill, for it is as incorruptible as a child who, still whole in spirit, will accept no compromises or excuses, and it will not stop tormenting us until we stop evading the truth." Dr Alice Miller

Chapter 2

The Inner Critic Part in Me

"If you gave your inner genius as much credence as your inner critic, you would be light years ahead of where you are now." Alan Cohen

WE BEGIN THE BOOK with the inner critic subpersonality because it is likely one of the most prominent and recognizable of the subpersonalities we will be exploring. As mentioned earlier, subpersonalities are an adaptation of our personality created typically as a means of protecting us. All parts exist on a continuum from very extreme to very mild. You can find parts anywhere along the spectrum. As therapists, we subscribe to the belief that our subpersonalities are parts of ourselves that we are meant to embrace, accept, love, and integrate rather than destroy, get rid of or run from, if we are to heal from what was responsible for creating them in the first place. You will notice a compassionate approach sprinkled throughout the book. Let us hold space for you as you begin to explore self-compassion.

You might recognize the inner critic as automatic negative thoughts. Its relentless destructive chatter is also described as negative self-talk. Our inner critic can be a harsh and deeply damaging force. Its strength and impact determine our overall mental wellbeing. The destructive voice in our heads is never satisfied, and it can spoil anything we may achieve, no matter how impressive. It magnifies the negative, spreading discontent in our lives.

Author Jena Pincott says, "*The paradox of the inner critic is that it attacks and undermines you in order to protect you from shame.*"

Let's delve into that critical voice that is always with you, like a monkey on your back.

The Voice Is Not You

The voice is a part of you with a specific purpose. Some refer to thoughts as "the monkey voice," or the part that reminds you of all the things you ought to be doing. Others use the metaphor of a monkey on your shoulder who pushes you to worry about everything. The message the voice sends is if you do this and that, you're prepared for any and every possible disaster.

While there is conflicting evidence about the number of thoughts we have daily, ranging from 6,000 to 60,000, the important part of that statement is that we have many, many thoughts every single day, and the majority of these are negative, attacking thoughts that feed the seed of self-doubt.

Have you ever been afraid to try a new activity, put a plan into action or reach for something that you truly desire with all your heart? We often sit on the sidelines of life because of the nagging voice that says, "You are not good enough." Many people experience voices, parts of themselves that are hostile and critical. The internal conflict is sometimes so strong that the person will even have difficulty carrying on with an ordinary routine and conversation. One factor that affects this conflict is how we deal with the voices or parts of the self.

Most approaches to helping people with the inner critic have something to do with either trying to get rid of the voice by taking medication until it fades away, or trying to ignore the voice altogether. It is important to note some people need to take medication to even begin to work with the inner critic. We recognize the value of pharmaceuticals and want to acknowledge that medication can be a piece of the wellness puzzle.

We also believe that interventions that explore the origin of the issue, create deeper and sustainable healing in the long run. It is the difference between putting a bandage on a bullet hole versus healing the wound from the inside.

There Is a Very Good Reason for the Inner Critic

A key aspect to working with hostile parts of the personality is to understand their function and the meaning behind their disruptive behaviours.

That critical voice in your head (and yes, we all have it) is not just a mean and nasty part of you that you can't control. You may perceive not having any control over it, especially at 3 o'clock in the morning as it is telling you that you have done everything wrong, that you shouldn't have said what you said in the meeting, that you will never amount to anything, or that there is no use trying to run a marathon or applying to college because you will surely fail.

Let's imagine you are a young child, and you are being your authentic self. You are completely attuned to your real self and carrying on according to that guidance system. You enter a store with your parent, and you see someone wearing flashy coloured clothing. You can't take your eye off of it because it's bright, it's fun and it's your favourite all-time colour. You point to the person and begin to giggle and start walking over towards the person, because you want to touch that flashy shirt. As you begin to walk towards the person, staring intently, you are yanked back by your parent, who tells you, "It's not polite to laugh at others," "Don't point, that's rude," "I've told you before, it's dangerous to talk to strangers. Stay close to me." We could keep going, but you get the gist. While this is an innocuous story, it helps us to understand what happens inside us. To a protective parent in the moment, it makes perfect sense to say all those things, because we understand our role to be that of protector and teacher, and we are likely doing the best we can given the life circumstances we are presented with. The child, however, may get the message that being excited about their favourite colour is a bad thing or that following their internal guidance system gets them in trouble and that their authentic self is not okay; therefore, the child must adapt in order to please those who love and care for them. Children want to please their parents as part of their attachment, and they learn over time that they must give up their authenticity in favour of their attachment to a parent.

"The way we talk to our children becomes their inner voice"
Peggy O'Mara

Over time, core beliefs are formed. Some common core beliefs are, "I am not good enough," "I am not important," "I am bad and not lovable." The original function of our core beliefs was to help us make sense of our experiences. However, they become unproductive or even harmful later in life. Harmful common core beliefs usually come in the form of rigid "*I am ...*" "*People are ...*" and "*The world is ...*" statements. It is in that sense that they are tied to our inner critics.

This is where the inner critic is created. Because we are not able to be ourselves, we must adapt our personality to fit our environment. In this scenario, a part may be created that serves as a reminder to the child that they are bad, they made a mistake, they are too friendly, and the list goes on. The purpose of this internal reminder (voice) may be to ensure that they stay in line instead of risking disapproval from a parent. When the inner critic is viewed from this point of view, it becomes an ally in protecting the child from pain.

Let's take a moment to reflect on this.

If we had a friend who pushed us out of traffic as an act of protection to avoid us being hit by a car, which would be very painful, it is likely that we would be eternally grateful to that person.

That leads us to this question: If our inner critic was created to keep us in line and out of harm's way, why are we not eternally grateful to it? Hmmm.... Interesting thought, isn't it?

Let's ask another question: If there are two people, one who is treated very harshly and critically and the other patiently and gently, which person is more likely to be responsive to a request?

Self-Compassion

It is important to discuss self-compassion before we delve more deeply into the chapters, because the act and practice of self-compassion doesn't seem to come naturally to us in our culture, yet it is no different than compassion for others. To have compassion, we must notice the suffering in another person. While most of us can demonstrate compassion towards others, turning compassion inward can seem quite foreign. We speak of this through our own experience and what we have observed with clients regarding the relationship between self and compassion.

Here is an example from Carmen and Suzanne's experience:

As leaders in the workplace, we have been rather supportive and understanding of staff's family and health needs, often saying when a staff needed to take time off, "do what you need to do to take care of your family," or when feeling ill, "go home and take care of yourself," or asking, "How can I support you?" We can easily support others with health and family needs because we wholeheartedly believe we show up at work as people with a plethora of human circumstances first and as workers/staff second. Because of this belief, it is quite natural for us to express compassion towards others. We also believe that unless we are able to attend to ourselves and our families, we will not be able to contribute to our work and our life in a meaningful way. As such, we have rarely felt that a staff member was not legitimately attending to themselves when taking time off. While we have supported others in taking time or taking care of themselves or their family members, we have not always been able to extend that same recognition of pain, suffering or ill-health in ourselves. There is a deeply-rooted belief that others need time to attend to themselves, but we don't. There is a belief and a voice that says, "You are weak when you take time for yourself; it is selfish." It is interesting to ask ourselves, how is it that we can believe that about ourselves yet not of others? This is just one of many examples where we and perhaps you notice a critical inner voice and have difficulty extending self-compassion. It is only in recognizing this belief in ourselves that we can make a different decision when that part of us is activated.

Perhaps because we recognize this behaviour in ourselves, we are often fascinated by our potential for compassion towards 8 billion people on the planet, yet when faced with the same set of circumstances, we are harsh and critical of ourselves and less than compassionate. Dr Kristen Neff's "*How would you treat a friend?*" approach is particularly effective for dealing with our inner critic. Neff asks us to imagine how we would interact with a struggling friend. What would you say to them? What tone of voice would you use? Next, we are invited to think of how we would tend to speak to ourselves, especially when we are struggling. Most of us will be truly shocked by the difference. Our goal is to speak to ourselves as caringly and kindly as we would speak to our friends.

We regularly use the "*How would you treat your friend?*" approach with clients, helping them expand their spectrum of possibility.

Compassion will come up time and again in this guidebook, and you will be regularly invited and encouraged to welcome self-compassion into your life as a pathway to healing. As you keep reading, notice areas in your life when you have been or are less than compassionate with yourself. Notice how you feel in those moments.

Our intention in this guide is not to convince you of our beliefs, but to have you reflect and experience possibilities that you may not have considered before. Take a moment to consider what it might be like the next time the inner critic says you can't write that book, or change careers, or go back to school, or take up weight training, or make that speech because you are too old, not fit enough, too busy, not good enough, or not strong enough. What if you were to notice its presence, embracing it and telling it how grateful you are that it has your back, instead of attempting to distract it by watching tv or drinking or internally telling it to shut up. Yes, we often tell the inner critic to be gone, and as you guessed, it doesn't listen.

Some people believe that regular meditation practice can help silence the inner critic and inspire us to be attentive to the messages of our hearts. Woven into that practice is self-love. Meditation teacher Sharon Salzberg, in her book *Real Love*, reminds us that meditation is one way to remember our innate goodness, with the idea that when we reflect on our positive traits, we build a bridge to a place of self-compassion and caring.

Taking the Wheel from the Inner Critic

Love it, thank it, and love it even more!

Our experience as a human being is a bit like driving a bus. Ideally, we would have our authentic self driving and navigating however that part of us is often occupying the back seat watching the scenery, enjoying the ride, and being witness to our interactions and circumstances as it patiently waits for the other parts to get out of the way so it can make its way to the driver's seat. The authentic self's patience is eternal, and it continues to be quite peaceful where it is. The purpose of embracing the inner critic is to help it relax and soften. Seeing the inner critic for what it is, attuning to it and giving it the attention it is so desperately seeking, helps to soothe it. The more we soothe it, the less attention it requires and the less control it has over our decisions and behaviour. Imagine having a wound on your finger and completely ignoring it and hitting the wound whenever you felt a twinge of pain. It's unlikely the wound would heal, and you might even notice that you adapt your activities based on the pain. Now imagine if you were to spend time caring for the wound, recognizing it as a part of yourself. You would find that over time, the wound heals as you soothe and nurture it. Our inner critic is no different.

Here are some ways your inner critic talks to you:

1. Blaming: It's your fault things go wrong.

2. Comparing: Why can't you be like her?

3. Setting unreasonable standards: It's not perfect, so start over.

4. Reminding you of your mistakes and failures: You never learn, do you?

5. Discouraging risks and change: You're going to fail anyway.

6. Brushing off wins: You were lucky.

7. "Shoulding": You should (not) be/do _____.

8. Insulting: You're dumb, weak, ugly.

9. Shaming: You're not good enough.

Even though it feels strange, converse with your inner critic and listen with empathy. Keep asking, *What's this really about?* or *What's underneath that?* until you find out its underlying fears. Get to your inner critic's heart, that feeling of vulnerability where walls have softened and defenses have lowered. Let yourself be seen.

"Courage starts with showing up and letting ourselves be seen." Brené Brown

Let's take a moment to reflect. Record anything that emerges:

_____
_____
_____
_____
_____
_____
_____
_____
_____
_____
_____

Carmen's Story

The year 2020 was a difficult year for most people, as we all struggled to accept and adjust to the Covid-19 pandemic. We can't escape uncertainty and unexpected life events, but it makes life more tolerable when we understand our inner critic. For the first ten months of the pandemic, I worked long and hard to meet the overwhelming needs of the people around me, in my family and in my business. I worked extra days and longer hours, slept less, ate more comfort food, and started to drink more wine. A part of me, the Rescuer (more in chapter 6), was driving the bus, on automatic pilot. I can remember the exact day I made the decision to change and how it electrified and terrified me with equal jolts. That day I stepped on the scales, and they tipped into a number my inner critic didn't like.

In this situation, my inner critic was my friend, suggesting that I needed to take better care of myself. My self-care had tanked in the pandemic, as I worked longer and harder. I listened to my inner critic with kindness and compassion. The message was true: I was tired, grumpy, and frumpy. As we entered 2021, I set out on a journey to correct my course and to nourish my body, mind, and soul. Running nourishes me in all three areas. Just as some people do yoga, paint, ride a horse or cook to find their calm experience and to understand how to live well, I run. I wanted to enter a deeper relationship with my body and to understand how to train it well. I wanted to see if I could run stronger and faster at the age of 55. More than that, I wanted to be healthy and strong so that I could be a kick-ass fun grandma, for at least a few more decades. My new intention was to live for several decades after 50, with the wisdom of my years and with the energy and strength I had in my 20s and 30s. The entire second half of my life, I vowed to seize fitness opportunities to be strong and helpful.

I threw myself into this new project because I was longing for flow and positive intention. Together, with my sister runners, we set a goal to complete a 30k race within the next few months. This is where I really got to know my inner critic and to practice what I preach. Befriending and loving my inner critic went from "*You are pudgy, menopausal, and already have too much on your plate. You can't possibly do this training.*" to "*Hey, sweet inner critic, don't you know I love a good challenge?*"

Winter running in Northern Canada is no joke. We ran in -30 degrees Celsius temperatures, snowstorms, and gusting winds with frozen eyelashes, hands and feet. We ran alone because of Covid restrictions, but we encouraged each other daily in our collective messenger chat. My inner critic would often chime in, especially when I slipped and fell on ice during a speed workout. "*Are you crazy? Are you trying to break a leg?*". "*Thank you, inner critic, for trying to keep me safe. I will be more careful next time.*" was the response. At last the frigid winter training was complete. The virtual race happened and the four of us finished the long and hilly race. Yay! Victory. "*Hey, inner critic, this is pretty big.*" I was a different person at the end of that race. I was stronger, both physically and mentally. Fitness and empowerment go hand in hand. On that same day in March, the four of us signed up for our first 42k marathon.

In early July, we started our marathon training. I laced up my new running shoes as my inner critic whispered in my ear, "*You are older, slower and definitely heavier than your running sisters. You don't have a runner's body, and you have fallen arches. Your flat feet can't run a marathon."* My initial response was to make up some excuse and to declare I was well beyond my athletic prime. Instead, I decided to tame my lion, my inner critic.

In many training runs, my inner critic would start to natter in my mind. *"You can't do this. Who do you think you are? Just quit, what are you trying to prove anyhow? You better bring your phone with you in case you can't finish."* When I got mad at these thoughts and tried to push them away, they got louder and stronger. I decided to remind my inner critic that when I run hard, I connect fully with my body and often push myself beyond what I thought possible.

I recognized this very familiar voice, which I have since named Debbie Downer. I am usually able to thank her for trying to protect me from failure, and I reassure her that I will listen to my body and not push myself beyond pain. Usually, the demon dialogues soften, and I finish my workout or run. I remind Debbie Downer that I am grateful to run with a great running community, Active Running, and all my running buddies.

Four weeks into training, life threw an unexpected curve ball at one of my running mates. *Pregnant! What?!* We were thrilled, excited and over the moon as this had been a big dream for many years. See, marathon training can create miracles! It was wonderful news, although Debbie Downer told me, *"It's a sign to quit and you should quit too! Get out now. Thank you, Debbie, I can't quit.",* was my response. Our training journey continued with some more of Debbie Downer's insults. At last, her roar was only a whisper and this part of me became tamer... until....

At week 8 of the training plan, the three of us set out for our longest training run of 34k. Debbie was whispering in the morning as I was nervous to embark on my longest run thus far. My inner critic started to get louder at 27k when my 47-yr-old running sister put in her ear buds, picked up her pace and went on her way. She was determined, fit as a fiddle and ran like a gazelle. *"You will never be as fast as her. You can quit and call it a day. Thank you, Debbie Downer but I have got this, slow and steady. I don't have to be as fast. This is not a race with my friend. This is a run for self-development, personal growth, and fun."* She agreed and got quiet. Yay. Dig deep, sister.

At 32k, my 49-yr-old friend picked up her pace for the intended 2k pick-up at the end of all training runs. She has wonderful pick-ups all the time. She is a feisty fit firecracker with driven intention. I struggled to pick up my pace. Debbie chimed in, *"There you go, you ran too fast again and now you don't have it in you to pick up for the last 2kms. You did it again. When will you learn?"* Again, I reminded my inner critic that this was not a competition. This was why I was practicing. I was learning how to pace. Debbie returned to a faint whisper and I mustered up a faster pace.

I finished my run knowing more about myself and what I am capable of in body, mind and spirit. This motivates me and spills into anything fulfilling my potential in this world. A long run pushes me outside the jagged edges of my comfort zone. In writing this book, I have also been in a race with myself, and now I hardly recognize the runner or the writer I was a year ago.

But let me take you back to when another part was driving my bus, when I was skeptical, tired, overworked, and pudgy. My inner critic nudged me, but we listen to each other with respect now. I invite you to join me in your journey toward getting to know your inner critic and to truly understand it, as you would your best friend. What is it trying to protect you from or save you from? I ran my first marathon with Debbie Downer as my new friend. She shifted from an inner critic to an inner nurturer. It takes time and practice to let go. So, don't beat yourself up when your inner critic chimes in. It might feel like an eternal 2-steps-forward-1-step-back process. And when you're super stressed or vulnerable, your inner critic can even flare up again. It's normal. Just keep going. In due time, you *will* transform your inner critic, and it'll become your ally.

You're not its victim anymore.

It does not matter whether you are a runner or do some other physical or non-physical activity, whether you are older or younger, male, female or other. For it is our greatest hope that your inner critic does not stop you from learning, growing, and living. Believe it or not, you are not broken or flawed. You have just believed your inner critic for too long. It is your turn to take the wheel. Do you want to take a course, apply for a new job, try something new or anything that seems too hard? It's OK to fail. In fact, it is a must. It is also our greatest hope that the REALignment practices will inspire you to chart your own individual path to wellness and return to real. You can feel worthy and discover who you really are.

Naming Your Inner Critic

You might want to name your inner critic something that resonates with you: *the bully, the troll, the judge, wolf, Darth Vader,* or anything else. Naming your inner critic separates you from it and creates the space to get to know it. Throughout the day, notice when your inner critic raises its voice: "*You can't do that. Remember what happened the last time? Oh, there goes Miss Know-It-All.*"

Whenever we recognize the voice of our inner critic, we may practice thinking, "*Thank you, inner critic.*" When it bombards us with unhelpful messages, we can decide not to take it too seriously. We may say, "*Here is Darth again, doing his job.*"

When we observe the inner critic in action, we may want to remind ourselves that our thoughts are just words and that our beliefs are just that: beliefs, not facts. They are nothing more than the unhelpful noise of our endlessly chattering minds. We are not those thoughts. We can defuse ourselves from them.

_____
_____
_____
_____
_____
_____
_____
_____
_____
_____
_____
_____

REALignment Practices

Sit quietly and notice how the mind constantly chatters. Then start noticing the spaces in between the chatter. At first, they will be tiny, almost imperceptible. Try to hold on to noticing the space. When your mind gets distracted and starts to chatter again, simply return your attention to the space between the chatter and hold it until you get distracted again. As you continue this practice, the spaces between the chatter will get longer and longer. This creates a quieter mind and creates space to be in the present.

_____
_____
_____
_____
_____
_____
_____
_____
_____
_____
_____
_____
_____
_____

Set a timer for 10 minutes and journal about a time when you demonstrated compassion to another person when they were going through something difficult. Describe what the situation was, what the other person thought about it, and what you said to or did for them. Then think about a time when you went through something similar. How did you act towards yourself? Were you compassionate or critical of yourself? Did you treat yourself with kindness or do anything that helped you feel cared for? Journal about this for 10 minutes, then notice if there are any differences and reflect on your answers. If you weren't kind to yourself, what could you do differently next time?

_____
_____
_____
_____
_____
_____
_____
_____
_____
_____
_____
_____

Have you ever stopped yourself from doing something because your inner critic said you weren't smart enough, strong enough, beautiful enough, kind enough? Find a quiet comfortable space, and close your eyes. Take three deep belly breaths, counting in to five, and out to five. Now, imagine you believe you are enough and try to sit with that feeling for 30 seconds. Observe what happens in your body when you sit with this feeling. Does your breathing change? Are there any physical sensations or a lack of sensations? Anything else that you notice in your body? Open your eyes and record what you experienced during this exercise. If this feels difficult or if 30 seconds seems too long, pretend you are just 5 or 10% more "enough" than you already feel and try to sit with that feeling for 5 to 10 seconds at a time. Journal about how it felt to be even a little more "enough." [This exercise can be practiced throughout the day minus the journaling.]

_____
_____
_____
_____
_____
_____
_____
_____
_____
_____
_____
_____
_____
_____
_____
_____

Make friends with your inner critic. Give it a name. Doodle or sketch what it looks like. Greet it when it shows up in your thoughts. "Hi, Princess Persnickety. You're here again. Thanks so much for watching out for me, but I've got this." Notice how doing this lessens the inner critic's grip on what you believe to be true and your own internal conflict.

Write down a crazy dream that you would love to accomplish or experience. Then make two columns on your paper. In the first column, write down everything your inner critic tells you about why you can't do it. Then in the second column, write down a response to the inner critic's objections [Use examples: 1 - You don't have the pick-up to do the last 2k. 2 - I may have been off-pace this time, but that's why I'm practicing so I can learn better pacing for future runs. 1 - I'll never have enough money to go on that trip. 2 - If I sit down and review my finances and make this trip a priority, I can make it happen.] Read over your list, and then, based on your responses in column 2, decide on a small step (even a tiny one!) you can take today to move you towards your dream. Commit to doing it.

Chapter 3

The People Pleaser Part in Me

"There's something very addictive about people-pleasing. It's a thought pattern and a habit that feels really, really good until it becomes desperate." Anne Hathaway

IT'S NOT AN ACCIDENT that we chose to discuss people pleasing on the heels of the inner critic exploration, as it is also another frequent theme in the therapy room and in our personal lives. Wherever you find yourself reading this, take a moment to recall a time when you put your own needs aside to please someone else. Every single one of us can find an example and more likely several examples. If we are to live harmoniously with other people on this planet, of course we need to compromise and be flexible and behave in ways that are pleasing to others. We wholeheartedly believe in and endorse kindness, flexibility, and compromise, but not at the expense of your health, well-being and authentic self. This is where it gets tricky and where we need to be aware of our tendencies and behaviours, because we must be able to distinguish between *"this is a really nice thing to do for someone because it makes me feel good"* and *"I need to put someone else's needs ahead of my own needs because I am not worthy or lovable otherwise."* The latter is rarely a conscious choice, and we often do not recognize that we are helping others at the expense of our own health and well-being.

The People Pleaser Part

Who doesn't love a nice person? We all want to be liked and loved, and for the most part, we have been taught and conditioned to be nice at any cost. Elvis Presley's song "Any Way You Want Me That's How I Will Be" is a great example of some of our early conditioning. While this song may not resonate with everyone, turn your ear to music over the last 50 years, and you will find that not much has changed. Many of us from our generation may have listened to this song and thought *"this must be how you show somebody you love them"*. You change to show someone else you love them. That's it! This is exactly how we lose our authentic selves.

Any Way You Want Me (That's How I Will Be)

Elvis Presley (written by Aaron Schroeder and Cliff Owens)

I'll be as strong as a mountain

Or weak as a willow tree

Anyway you want me

That's how I will be

I'll be as tame as a baby

Or wild as the raging sea

Anyway you want me

That's how I will be

In your hand my heart is clay

To take and mold as you may

I'm what you make me, you've only to take me

And in your arms I will stay

I'll be a fool or a wise man

My darling you hold the key

Yes, anyway you want me

That's how I will be

I will be

Contrary to the belief that we must change to please others, we are not stuck in a world where we have to be people pleasers in order to be loved. We do not have to be *any way you want me* to be loved and accepted, but that's the story we have been told and now believe. On the surface, pleasing people may seem harmless. After all, what's wrong with making other people happy? We love being helpful, kind and considerate, and it makes us really happy to brighten someone's day. Perhaps you strive for peace and harmony in your relationships, and you routinely put others before yourself. Others can count on you to "take one for the team." After all, self-sacrifice is part of your nature.

If you have a people pleaser part, you often try to be who others want you to be (just like the song), to agree with them, and to fit in. You may not be consciously aware that you are doing this, but there is a part of you that wants to please others in order to avoid reactions that you are afraid of. We're wired to need others, which is why rejection is so painful. But we have the power to grow from it and recover. Just like healing a body part, such as an injured leg, we can also heal our people pleaser parts.

In the words of Pink, "*Oh, the bone breaks. It grows back stronger.*"

Strong Bones and Strong Boundaries Are Beautiful!

One major problem with pleasing people is a complete lack of boundaries. Saying yes to everyone else can unfortunately mean saying no to yourself. What can start as a simple desire to be nice can lead to a cascade of overwhelm and neglect of your own needs. It's almost as if you become so hyper-focused on everyone else that you completely forget yourself.

Does this sound familiar? Many times, in life, the needs of those around us take priority, and we slowly lose ourselves and let go of our interests. Our needs took a back burner as we put out the fires of everyone else around us. Unfortunately, when we slowly assume responsibility for the thoughts and feelings of those around us, our mindset turns decidedly more negative. Without boundaries, we start to resent those around us for all the work we are doing and the work they're not doing. This can quickly transform into resentment and passive-aggressive thoughts, feelings, and actions. A lack of boundaries is the fast track to overwhelm, burnout, and stress.

The Mind-Body Connection

There is more and more scientific evidence emerging regarding the link between mind and body. We can't ignore this any longer, and we encourage you to pay attention to times in your life when your emotional state has impacted your physical state. We have all heard the saying, "If you don't make time for your health, you will be forced to make time for illness." This is especially true when discussing the people pleaser part of ourselves, which is always preoccupied with the needs of others while denying its own needs. Dr. Gabor Maté in his book *When the Body Says No* discusses the link between our emotional selves and the body and how disease may be the body's way of saying no to what the mind won't acknowledge. We highly recommend this book for you if you are interested in learning more about the impacts of stress on the body and how certain personality traits may put us at risk of disease.

We raise the mind-body connection in this chapter because when we neglect our own needs in favour of caring for others or pleasing others, we literally prematurely age. This is not to say that we should not care for others; indeed, awareness of how we care for others is important in caring for ourselves. Dr. Gabor Maté observed that people diagnosed with certain chronic diseases had similar personality traits, which put them at risk of disease. One of these traits is that of caring for the needs of others while ignoring your own needs. This is an area that touches Suzanne very deeply. Here is an example from her life: I come from a long history of women conditioned to put their needs secondary to those of their loved ones. Stories of my grandmother standing behind my grandfather ready to serve his every need as he ate his dinner are often discounted as a sign of the era. While there may be truth to that, we must also recognize that her entire life was dedicated to serving his every need at the expense of her needs, This is the legacy she passed on to her daughters. She died at the age of 55 of a rare form of cancer. Fast-forward to 2018, when my aunt was dying of a rare neurological disorder and lung cancer (a non-smoker all her life). She was so proud of always being there for those who needed her. She died at the age of 61. While we can't predict illness and death, I wonder if there is a connection between their premature deaths and their extreme people pleasing parts. As people and as a society, we value selflessness, yet we now have growing evidence that caring for others ahead of ourselves is making us sick and even potentially killing us.

Your Early Years - The Birth of the People Pleaser

As with all parts of your personality, your early years had something to do with your current people pleasing pattern. If your parents were overly critical, or emotionally/physically unavailable, your young self may have adapted a people pleasing coping mechanism. Being feminist-era moms, we don't want mothers and women (or men) to bear so much responsibility or ultimate blame if things go wrong. Certainly, many other factors other than mothering and parenting shape a child's life.

While doing research over the years, we have read many books on attachment and the parent-child bond. These books are often not intended to blame or shame parents or ourselves for mistakes or mishaps. They are about understanding our personality parts so we can course-correct. We believe almost all parents harbour good intentions toward their children. Unfortunately, some parents do not translate those good intentions. In an imperfect world, even well-intentioned parents can be flawed and an innocent child harmed. Once we accept this reality, we can start to address the people pleasing part we have developed throughout our lives. Say hello to hope and goodbye to denial.

Perhaps you learned early on that if you were "helpful" and "agreeable" then people loved and accepted you. Because we are incapable of caring for ourselves when we are young, we depend upon others to care for us. The people-pleasing part plays proactive and protective roles. This part works hard to manage and prevent painful or traumatic feelings and experiences from flooding one's consciousness. The part's purpose is to protect us from being overwhelmed emotionally by feelings of shame, pain, loneliness, and rejection.

Quicksand

People pleasing often means you are suppressing your feelings. Your calendar is packed to the brim with activities you may not be over the moon about. It may be so full that you feel as if adding even one more task would absolutely put you over the edge of sanity. You're constantly running and spinning your wheels, but you never feel as if you get anywhere as you sink deeper and deeper into quicksand. Feeling stuck is no joke. The people pleasing part has driven the bus into deep trouble. You are stuck in the quicksand and sinking fast!

Honouring our needs is usually neglected in the name of self-sacrifice. In fact, you may be completely unable to identify activities that would be good for you because you're too busy meeting everyone else's needs. You have zero free time and no hope that you ever will in the future. Does this seem familiar to you? When was the last time you looked at your schedule against activities that light you up? Can you recall a time when you suppressed your feelings, anger, and sadness because it was inconvenient to others?

Let's take a moment to reflect on this. Use the space below to jot down what emerges:

_____
_____
_____
_____
_____
_____
_____
_____
_____
_____
_____
_____
_____
_____

Self-Worth

Another word for self worth is self-esteem and is defined as an internal sense of being good enough and worthy of love. Self-esteem is vital to our wellbeing. Healthy self-worth includes valuing our own needs.

Constantly worrying about the needs of others often means you will completely forget your own needs. As your own needs sink lower and lower on your ever-growing list of things to do, so will your self-worth. You begin to believe that everyone else's needs are more important than your own, which only serves to plummet your self-worth.

As your self-worth decreases, so does the quality of your relationships. Excessive people-pleasing often means you've completely lost touch with who you are as a person. Being authentic and real is the very thing that can strengthen relationships with others.

Control and Predictability

At its core, pleasing people can also be about control. Taking control feels safe and predictable because this is likely a long-standing pattern for you. It's a pattern in which you subconsciously assume responsibility for the emotions of others around you and act accordingly. But you can break free.

Burnout

Burnout can happen to anyone. It is particularly common amongst people pleasers who have been taught to believe that they should be able to handle an extraordinary amount of stress and responsibility while being an exemplary soccer mom with a clean house. Burnout is very difficult, exhausting and most of all confusing because it is possible to love your life and still experience burnout! It is possible to be a highly experienced person and still have burnout sneak up on you.

Signs of burnout include loss of engagement, resulting in lack of motivation, which can take an emotional and physical toll. It sometimes feels like a constant dull ache, or it can feel like swimming against the current on a stormy day.

Burnout Recovery

Burnout recovery is about moving through the experience and getting to understand how your people pleasing tendencies contribute to this feeling. Avoiding, denying, or putting a bandage on the symptoms can just make it worse. In this way, it's important that we do not treat our people-pleasing part as an enemy because it has a protective purpose. The symptoms of burnout alert us to our people pleasing part, which needs attention. Listening to this signal can be a critical turning point.

We believe in approaching our people-pleasing part with compassion and treating burnout as a messenger that has important information to communicate and share. Individual experiences of burnout will have important messages about changes that need to be made in one's own life. And so, burnout recovery and burnout prevention often start with listening, giving yourself space to understand your experience, and focusing on one change at a time.

One change at a time also means one breath at a time. So, take a deep breath, and slowly exhale....

Let's take a moment to reflect. What messengers are showing up in your life? Do you recognize yourself in anything you have read in this chapter? Using the space below, write down one change you are willing to make for yourself.

_____
_____
_____
_____
_____
_____
_____
_____
_____
_____
_____

REAL Stories

Hearing the unique ways others have experienced their subpersonalities can be helpful in remembering you are not alone in this journey. If you find yourself asking "is it just me?," please know it isn't. You may recognize yourself or parts of yourself in some of these stories.

Enrique

Enrique's wife tells him that she is upset because he isn't spending enough time with her. Enrique immediately feels horrible, and he tries to figure out how to spend more time with her, although he is already stretched too thin with trying to please his boss. He never gets curious about whether her perception is real or if her demands are reasonable. He doesn't ask himself how attentive he actually is, or whether she needs a lot of attention because of her own insecurities. His only thought is: *How can I please her? How can I get her to stop being upset with me?* He tries to remember to give her more attention, but he hasn't even figured out what the problem is!

Ginette

During our first session, Ginette told me that she felt like shouting from a rooftop, "*I will do anything for love!*" She recalled always trying to please her parents, but one story from her childhood was particularly telling. One day in a department store, she noticed her mother looking at a particular lipstick, and she understood how much her mother wanted it. She vowed to somehow get it for her, even though she was only 9 years old. She saved her milk money from school for many weeks until she was able to afford the lipstick. She wrapped it in a beautiful picture she had carefully painted. She eagerly waited for her mom to open the gift but was crushed with her reaction. Her mother accused her of stealing and sent her to her room without supper.

Garett

Garett came to therapy after two failed marriages. He could never get his father's approval. His father was an accomplished athlete and a physical education teacher. Garett strived to be like his father and older brother, who were natural athletes. Although he spent years in golf lessons, ran track and tried every sport known to mankind, he could never reach the level of success his father and older brother experienced. He could never live up to his parents' expectations. He decided that maybe his choice of an athletic girlfriend would make them happy. "When I met her, I thought, wait till my family meets her. They will love her and be happy I chose her." He was hoping that he would finally get the approval he longed for. However, after meeting her, they expressed disappointment as she did not meet their standards. Garett has spent his entire life looking for partners that please his parents.

Sandra

Sandra attended counselling to process the deep grief experienced at the recent and sudden passing of her best friend. Sandra expressed having experienced several losses in the last 5 years and was really struggling with this most recent one. She had been the caregiver for many of these family members ahead of their passing. She described herself as a natural caregiver, a professional woman always on top of her game and in control of her life. People came to her for support and advice; she was the strong one, but the passing of her best friend rocked her world. She was experiencing significant physical issues; lack of appetite, foggy thinking and sleeping 12-14 hours per day. These are all expected symptoms following a significant loss. Interestingly, she described herself as a naturally kind, supportive, and giving person. "*I don't want to toot my own horn,*" she said, "*but I have always been quite selfless,*" and then she went on to say that following the passing of her friend and after ensuring that everything was taken care of, including making sure that everyone else was okay, she went home and collapsed. The care of others over her own physical, emotional, psychological, and spiritual needs had brought her to her knees.

Interestingly, as a society, we proudly show our badge of honour at having sacrificed our own wellbeing in favour of others.

Let's remember that children with unmet emotional needs, such as belonging, keep trying to please, hoping to gain love and respect even years later.

What Is Your Story?

Perhaps you have learned that people like other people who agree with them, even if only superficially. Rather than risk rocking the boat and possible rejection, you simply say yes to everything. After all, we need our attachment for survival.

You may be seeking approval and validation from others rather than looking internally for your value. This leads to a constant cycle of people pleasing as you seek outside affirmation about your worth, which is lacking from within. This ultimately means you end up believing that you need to prove your worthiness to others or face rejection.

Our self-worth affects how we interpret other people's behaviour. If our self-esteem is shaky, we are more likely to be reactive to signs of disfavour in our relationships. Our people pleaser part will take over and drive our bus.

Let's take a moment to reflect on your story. Using the space below, write what you notice about your people pleaser part:

_____
_____
_____
_____
_____
_____
_____
_____
_____
_____
_____
_____
_____

Acceptance, Attachment and Love

Both young and adult children want to please their parents and feel their approval. Beginning early in life, it is important for children to receive attention, love, and approval. However, the approval must be for who we are authentically, not for what our parents want us to be. Although you may have developed the people-pleasing coping mechanisms as a young child, you are now an adult. You have control over your own life now, and you can choose to make positive changes, especially if your current mindset isn't working for you.

Befriending the People Pleaser Part

By this time in the chapter, you may have gained some additional insights into what people pleasing entails and where it comes from. It's time now to befriend and honour this part that has possibly kept you safe from harm for years.

Listen with Compassion

If you've been living your life for others, it will take time and practice to be kind to yourself. Start small and pay attention to that small voice inside.

Notice your feelings and notice bodily sensations, instead of shoving them deep down. How are you feeling right now? Are you authentically living a life you love? Or are you living the life everyone else wants for you? How does it truly feel to say yes to something? Does doing what you agreed to do make you feel energized and alive? Does it align with your core purpose? Or does it leave you feeling tired and drained?

Practice identifying your smallest, most basic needs. Once identified, imagine (visualize) what it would feel like to have your needs met. Thank this part and practice saying no with kindness to expectations. NO, can be a difficult word. You're so used to pleasing everyone around you that it may sound harsh and uncaring. But as fellow people pleasers, we can say with certainty that saying no to others means saying yes to yourself.

Start by identifying something on your list of activities that you truly don't want to do. Something that is a huge imposition to yourself or that causes extensive anxiety. Think about how great it would feel not to have that thing looming over your head anymore. How amazing would it be to get back just a little of your time and freedom? Pretty incredible, right? Returning to your real self is about honouring your needs.

Re-examining your Life Since the Global Pandemic

We all took a mandated pause. It was beyond our control. We didn't have to say yes or no, or make many social decisions. The pendulum has now shifted, most restrictions have lifted, we are re-entering the world and people now seem to be experiencing decision fatigue. It's a combination of a sudden surge of events and bearing the weight of making many new decisions. You may notice your people pleaser part becoming more active and perhaps driving your bus again. For some with strong people pleaser parts, the global pandemic offered a perfect reason for not making unrealistic commitments to others, and you may have noticed that your people-pleaser part took a bit of a break.

Let's take a moment to reflect on how your people pleaser part was affected by the pandemic. Using the space below, record what emerges for you:

_____
_____
_____
_____
_____
_____
_____

We too share the anxiety of navigating a complex world with competing priorities. Now, more than ever, is the time to befriend our people pleaser part. How do you want to show up in the next chapter of your life?

Our answers inform our decisions and actions. Self-reflection is one of the best tools we have developed for setting boundaries. We are all built differently on the extrovert and introvert scale, yet we are wired for connection and belonging. After the recent isolating experience we have lived through, it is more important than ever to take care of ourselves.

Take a deep breath, and let's do some breathing. Breathe deeply for four seconds, hold for four seconds, breathe out for four seconds, and hold for four seconds. Repeat as many times as feels comfortable.

Let's not go back and do some of the same stuff that didn't work in the first place. Let's not buy into the temptation to go on auto-pilot because it is a safe place and it is what we know. We too have made the mistake of allowing ourselves to reach the threshold of overwhelm so many times. Like you, we are learning to honour our true feelings and our yes's and our no's.

Ask yourself the following questions:

Think of a situation in your life that is creating stress. Do I need to say yes or no? Why? Do I want to do it or not do it? Why?

_____
_____
_____
_____
_____
_____
_____
_____
_____
_____
_____
_____

REALignment Practices

Reflect on a time when you changed something fundamental about yourself to please someone else. You may have been looking for a parent, a partner, a teacher or a friend's approval. How did this make you feel? How familiar was this feeling or how far back does this feeling go? Journal or doodle what is coming up for you?

Take a look at your calendar and identify at least one obligation you can let go of. Look at each of your appointments and notice what comes up in your body.

Are there any sensations or temperature changes? Where do you feel it? What do you think these physical signals tell you about your obligation? Use them to gauge whether you enjoy each task or you're doing it to keep someone else happy. From there decide if there is anything you can let go of. Keep it simple.

_____
_____
_____
_____
_____
_____
_____
_____
_____
_____
_____
_____
_____
_____
_____

If telling someone you are backing out of an obligation feels like too much, practice by using your voice to express what you want. Start small - the next time someone asks you where you want to eat or what kind of take-out to get, say what you want right away instead of saying you don't care or asking them to choose. Notice how it feels in your body to state your needs firmly and politely. Sink into it and stay there for at least 5 seconds. The next time you are asked your opinion try to remember this feeling before you reply. As you slowly start to make your own needs known and have them met, notice if any nagging, chronic physical ailments change over time - things like migraines, irritable bowel syndrome, allergies, anxiety, or eczema.

Have they stayed the same, worsened, or improved? What else do you notice? Remember to notice with compassion and curiosity.

Chapter 4

The Perfectionist and the Expert Parts of Me

"Perfectionism is self-abuse to the highest order." Anne Wilson Schaef

THE CURSE OF PERFECTION. Perfectionism in psychological terms can be defined as the need to be perfect or to appear to be perfect, or even to believe that it's possible to achieve perfection. We tend to view perfectionism as something to aspire to, a positive trait of sorts. Everywhere we look we see messages of needing to be perfect in some way or another. We have created this image of ourselves and of our world that perfection is possible. Take a moment to think about magazine covers, whether it's fashion, home renovations, parenting or food magazines. Everything looks perfect, and the message is if you don't look like this or have this, you are not good enough. Perfectionism in our culture is seen as something to reach for. Your internal protective part is relentless in its efforts towards perfection, and you are also bombarded with societal messages that promote the illusion of perfection. The ingredients for a perfect storm.

Perfectionism is a protective mechanism we employ to ensure we don't get hurt. We believe that perfection protects us from experiencing blame, ridicule, and criticism, which is why we strive to work, live, look and be perfect. We use it as a shield from pain. At some point in your life, likely in your early years, you developed a belief that you were not good enough or worthy enough, and you recognized that the recipe to avoiding ridicule, embarrassment and shame was to be perfect in the eyes of others. That is a heavy load to carry.

It's a Myth

Yes, being perfect is a myth! In fact, buying into and perpetuating the myth is harmful to ourselves and others as we set unrealistic expectations that can never be met. Those with perfectionist traits often experience stress, anxiety, and obsessive behaviours because of the immense pressure they place on themselves and others to be perfect and to live perfectly. They are highly critical, beating themselves up over any indication that their standard has not been met. There can also be fear that if they don't shoot for perfection, they will become low-achievers and not reach their goals. Perfectionism can greatly diminish our self-esteem, enjoyment of life, and sense of peace, as it can lead to extensive stress, fear of judgement, and worries of inadequacy.

There are different categories of perfectionism we're vulnerable to. Let's begin with the internal desire to be perfect; let's call that self-led perfectionism. Setting high standards for ourselves and wanting to do our very best can be a good thing as it allows us to meet our potential if we recognize our strengths and limitations. There is nothing wrong with wanting to do a good job, and this type of perfectionism would not be considered maladaptive unless we attach our self worth to the outcome.

External-oriented perfectionism is the desire to live up to others' expectations, comparing ourselves to the achievements and accomplishments of others. There is tremendous pressure associated with this type of perfectionism often leading to anxiety because the person can never live up to what society expects.

A third way the perfectionist part may show up in your life is by holding others to unrealistic expectations. When we become critical and judgemental of others, we often place expectations on them. This type of perfectionism might force someone to never delegate any work or to always want to do everything themselves because what others do never measure up. This behaviour may cause significant stress and pressure because of the belief that they are the only ones who can perform or do something.

Experiencing external-oriented perfectionism or putting pressure on others may lead to exhaustion or burn out. If you recognize this in yourself, take a moment to explore your drivers.

Let's take a moment to reflect on this. Do you recognize yourself in anything you have read in this chapter? Use the space below to jot down what emerges:

_____
_____
_____
_____
_____
_____
_____
_____

Shame

"When perfectionism is driving, shame is always riding shotgun and fear is the annoying voice in the back seat." Brené Brown

We cannot talk about perfectionism without talking about shame, because shame always accompanies perfectionism. We highly recommend reading any of Brené Brown's books or listening to her podcast as, in our view, she is an expert in the field of shame.

Shame damages the self-image like no other emotion can. Shame is a deeply held sense of feeling bad to the core, and it can involve self-loathing and self-contempt. Shame can be a part of your felt-self, and it can often be felt viscerally. While guilt can at times improve your well-being, as it motivates you towards a particular direction, shame does not.

For some, no matter how successful, kind, attractive and smart they are, it is still not good enough and creates the rise of shame, which sounds like this: *"You are not good enough. You are not enough. You must do better."*

"If I look perfect, do it perfect, work perfect and live perfect, I can avoid or minimize shame, blame and judgment." Brené Brown

Shame is not resolved through verbal persuasion or cognitive approaches. Shame needs to be spoken to from the heart and held with acceptance, understanding and compassion if it is to heal.

Striving for Excellence vs Perfectionism

There is nothing wrong with having high standards. In fact, it can make us achieve great things in life, and not everyone who does things well is a perfectionist. As mentioned earlier, there is a difference between an internal drive to do things well and a need to be perfect for others. One is tied to your authentic, self-led part, which is internally satisfied with a particular level of quality or excellence, while the other is present to avoid rejection and pain. It is important to recognize the difference. In which areas of your life do you enjoy something done well, and in which areas are you vulnerable to perfectionist behaviour? Take a moment to jot down what emerges:

_____
_____
_____
_____
_____
_____
_____
_____
_____
_____

Suzanne's Story

I love to cook gourmet meals, spending hours reading recipes and planning the perfect Christmas menu, using the best ingredients and techniques. I regularly try new recipes and seek feedback for improvements. I push myself to create new and better-tasting foods all the time. The joy I experience from looking at a well-set table with a wide assortment of dishes, all deliciously prepared and pleasing to the palate, is immeasurable. It makes me want to create an even better dish the next time. While there is satisfaction in receiving accolades from family and friends who have just enjoyed a wonderful meal, the real joy comes from knowing I have executed a delicious dish and am getting better and better at my craft. I can feel the joy in my heart as I write about it. Conversely, when my children were young and in school, I insisted on making them gourmet lunches. At the time, I believed I did this because I loved to prepare lunches (who loves to make lunches? NO ONE, ever!) and wanted the kids to have a healthy balanced meal. The truth about preparing fabulous lunches, as I look back on it (and knew to some degree at the time) was my insecurity as a parent. If my children showed up at school with a perfectly balanced, home-cooked lunch, it meant I was a good parent in the eyes of the teachers and the other parents. This was my shield to cover my shame at being an imperfect parent who yelled at her kids and was regularly angry at them. Their perfect lunch, the homemade-only standard I held, was my way of showing others that I was a better parent than my ex-husband. My outward appearance of being a perfect parent protected me from the guilt and shame of my imperfection...or so, I thought.

I'll Do It Later

Procrastination can be a symptom of perfectionism. Do you identify as someone who procrastinates? Those with perfectionist tendencies can get caught up and overwhelmed in the planning of a task or project, and because their standards are so unrealistic, they often cannot even begin to execute the task because their standard is not attainable. It can be a vicious cycle because procrastination can create stress and anxiety, which further heightens our nervous system. If the goal is perfection, the sense of overwhelm can paralyze you. We have seen this, especially in work settings, where the underlying message is to get the job done well within very short timelines.

Sometimes a perfectionist's fear of failure is so terrifying that they procrastinate because they would rather not do something at all if it can't be done perfectly.

Carmen's Story

How does our true nature express itself? As an example, Carmen has a push-forward nature, and likes to get things done, with an eye for perfectionism. I have a natural tendency to step back, see the bigger picture or balcony perspective, and I know how to perfect it in my mind's eye. I can see the outcome without really knowing how to get there. I struggle with the most important steps on the dance floor, or the tiny steps it takes to achieve my big balcony perspective. (The devil is in the details!) This is just my true nature.

My natural perfectionism tendency was further developed in my childhood. I was a determined child by nature, and I learned how to survive in an unpredictable environment. I learned that leaning into perfectionism brought some positive results but the downside is constant striving and exhaustion. Attempting to be good at certain hobbies could sometimes bring peace and harmony or a distraction from my environment. My perfectionist part can show up as competition in sports events. It can show up in the way I colour code my calendar and arrange my closet, and in the expectations, I place on myself. So, what happens when I can't control my environment or my life situations? I lean into perfectionism, or what I perceive as control.

Lipstick on the Delivery Table

This story is for all the girls out there who were afraid to claim their power, thinking that society would look down upon them and shame them for not being perfect. This is all of us who miss bids for connection in the present moment because we are thinking about what is next.

It was midnight in the early 90's, when my water broke five weeks early. I had returned home that afternoon, after spending three weeks in the hospital on complete bed rest. I was home for approximately eight hours. I was anxious, nervous, and panicked when I climbed into our vehicle, wondering if my babies would be OK. Would my twins be taken from me and flown to a neonatal unit in a city far away?

When we reached the hospital, I discovered my obstetrician was not on-call. I did not know who would be delivering my babies. I collapsed in the hallway as my legs gave out underneath me. The lights were dim, and I barely noticed nurses rushing around me. I could feel an endless churning rumbling deep inside, the butterflies in my stomach, sweaty palms, and I could hardly breathe. Panic struck. Nothing was going according to my perfect detailed plan—the birthing movie I had played over and over in my mind.

My (then) husband, head down with pen to paper, diligently and magnificently recorded every contraction, every pause, and every groan for the next five hours. He was managing his anxiety the best way he knew how, by paying attention to detail and recording it. Why wasn't he talking to me? Why wasn't he rubbing my back or helping me breathe? I looked out the window and thought about leaving, *"Just crawl out the window,"* but I was trapped. I reached for my purse beside my bed. My lipstick! Such a beautiful and perfect shade of pink. I couldn't control who would deliver my premature babies, my husband's personal calming actions, or the chaos and hustle and bustle around me, but I could apply lipstick!

When my beautiful twin girls were born at 5:20 a.m. and 5:29 a.m. they were whisked away into incubators. It was both the most terrifying and the most beautiful experience in my life. The 6 hour wait to meet them and hold them felt like an eternity. I could only hold them through the arm pockets in the incubators. When I felt powerless to control my situation, my perfectionist part took the wheel and did the only thing it could in that moment, it gave me lipstick. It sounds completely ludicrous, vain and unrelated, but this can be how our parts show up.

Perfectionism is often associated with vulnerability and a lack of resilience. What is more vulnerable than delivering twins in a room with mostly strangers? My perfectionist part was on high alert, very aware that I could not control anything. Yet my perfectionist part wanted to hide my shame, fear and vulnerability. I realize now that my perfectionist part was trying to help me feel some sense of control in a situation I had absolutely no control over. My fear was raw, and I didn't know what to do.

Thirty-two years later, I can reflect on the birth of my babies and understand that my twenty-five-year-old self was terrified and alone. My perfectionist part, I now call Gertrude, tried to protect me from shame and not being enough. Today, Gertrude will often relax and begin to trust me when I hold her with compassion and kindness. She tries to protect me from a very vulnerable part of me that was judged, rejected, and dismissed—a part of me that could not control my environment.

We can all access this part of ourselves and heal it. Perfectionistic behaviour may be an attempt to compensate for the underlying core belief of feeling inadequate or not good enough. Striving to do things well can be healthy when satisfaction is gained through the effort to succeed. Perfectionists tend not to be happy with their accomplishments and thus have strongly developed inner critics. Imperfection is part of being human. Failures and mistakes are opportunities to learn and grow if we view them as an opportunity. (P.S. I still love lipstick!)

Fear of Failure

In some instances, this drive for progress or improvement can be a positive force. Think about the way an athlete trains using deliberate practice to hone in on every tiny detail of their skill. Here is another example of Carmen's experience with her perfectionist part. As I trained for my first marathon, I got to know both my inner critic and my inner perfectionist. Setbacks or failures aren't "all or nothing" situations. They're opportunities to reflect, learn, and adjust your approach. I set a goal to complete my first marathon in 4 hours and 30 minutes. Did I reach this perfect goal? No. I finished my race in 4 hours and 43 minutes. Did I fail? Does 13 minutes over my target make me a failure? My perfectionist part would say, "*Hell yes!*" I could have easily gone down that path and beaten myself up, and for a few seconds, I did just that. The disappointment quickly faded when I invited my inner nurturer to the party. "*I did it. I completed my first marathon. I did it!*" I allowed my true emotions to bubble up and stream down my face. I gave myself permission to take it all in. A year later, I ran my second marathon with the same goal of 4 hours and 30 minutes. Did I reach this goal the second time? No. I missed it by 4 minutes. Did I enjoy the race? Absolutely! It's about progress, not perfection!

Few of us see failures in the same light. Instead, we use what therapists call "maladaptive perfectionism," which involves collecting a manuscript of all the moments when we didn't succeed and revisiting them on a regular basis. This causes us to raise the bar even higher, increasing the likelihood of failure.

But what if our book of failures wasn't a place for shame and judgment? When you see failure as simply a launching place for success, you break out of the need to be perfect, and you can understand that each mistake is a step towards something better. Good is the enemy of great. But perfect is the enemy of everything.

We all fall into perfectionism from time to time. You are not perfect, and you will never be perfect. You are better than that. You are human, and you are imperfectly perfect. When we accept that we're allowed to make mistakes (and that some of the best products and ideas of all time came from screw-ups), we not only feel less stressed, but we give ourselves permission to experiment, explore, and create. We allow ourselves to return to real. When our perfection part softens through our self-compassion, our authentic selves emerge, and we can achieve our goals and make our dreams a reality.

"No matter what gets done and how much is left undone, I AM ENOUGH. It's going to bed at night thinking, yes, I am imperfect and vulnerable and sometimes afraid, but that doesn't change the truth that I am also brave and worthy of love and belonging." Brené Brown

REALignment Practices

Practice feeling that you are enough. Take 4 slow, deep breaths. Close your eyes if it is helpful to do so. Feel into the thought that you are enough just as you are with every fibre of your being for 5-10 seconds. Notice how it feels in your body to believe you are enough. Is there a release of tension, a lowering of shoulders, a sense of calm? See if you can do this once or several times a day. Then try to slowly build up to feeling enough for 30 seconds to 1 minute at a time several times a day. Every time you do this exercise make sure to notice any physical sensations in your body. Keep revisiting this exercise and compare your results over time.

Reflect on a time in the past when a perceived failure was a step toward where you truly needed to go. Did you not get the dream job, did a relationship break down, or was something you made rejected for publication or exhibition? Journal whether this event sent you on a trajectory, that in retrospect, was exactly where you needed to go and if everything worked out in the end. Also, reflect on what you learned from this experience and how it helped you grow as a person.

_____
_____
_____
_____
_____
_____
_____
_____
_____
_____
_____
_____
_____

The Expert

"I became an overachiever to get approval from the world."
Madonna

By now, you may notice that our subpersonalities are endless, and that you are truly unique. A close friend to the perfectionist part is the expert part. This subpersonality can be described by the need to try to do everything all the time with exceedingly high standards.

For example, when we are not the ideal partner, worker, manager, colleague, parent, and more, the feeling of guilt takes over. That nagging voice can say, "*I need to know more about that topic. I wish I had acted on my instinct to make that report better. I'm not a good partner for not cooking a homemade dinner tonight, even though I am exhausted.*"

Learning, growing, and improving are often positive experiences. They are truly important parts of being human. However, the expert part needs to accomplish and get things done at the cost of burnout and fatigue. It has to "do" rather than "be." When this subpersonality is driving our bus, we sometimes forget to sit still. This contributes to the unhealthy cycle of feeling guilty about not being able to do it all, be it all, and have it all.

Much like our people-pleasing and perfectionism patterns, when we get hooked into other people's expectations, it can be a tiring dance. Often there is a belief that we must do this or that to be seen and loved. We want to make people proud, and do our best, but unless we check in and ask, "*Is this really what I want?*", we get caught in everyone's expectations but our own. We get trapped in the cycle of doing rather than just being. It's very easy to forget that our best performance and our best thinking comes from being, rather than doing. Anyone who has an expert part is always wanting to be better, always wanting to get there, always wanting to climb the next rung of the ladder. Our world needs experts to solve problems, to find a cure for cancer, to send rockets into space, and to solve world hunger. It's absolutely positive to have expertise in an area that lights you up. But do you know when enough is enough? How do you decide?

Carol's Story

I Try So Hard! Carol, a high-achieving person embarked on a whirlwind of accomplishments and achievements. She decided at a very young age that working hard was the only way to feel good about herself and to compensate for the belief "*I am not enough.*" She wanted to prove to her mother and to others just how good she could be. "*I am worthy because of my titles and the impressive accomplishments I obsess over.*" Carol finds it difficult to love herself for just being real. She bases her worth on her expertise and titles. The high achiever becomes a "human doing" rather than a "human being." Carol came to therapy with burnout and adrenal fatigue. To the outside world, she appeared to be Wonder Woman, but she was slowly dying inside. Constantly looking for more things to improve had created a vicious cycle of over-functioning and crashing into under-functioning.

Are you like Carol? One easy way to think about this is to look at how you define yourself. Take a moment to reflect and jot down the words you use to describe yourself. For example, we might choose driven, incompetent, confident, fit, fat, lazy, or more. The words we use and identify with help us determine if we are self-led or led by a protective part of ourselves.

Is there a me to like without my accomplishments? What do we really mean when we say, I like myself? Are you someone who knows what it is like to really like others, or find things that are likeable in others? Can we do this with regards to ourselves in ways that are not hijacked by inadequacy and shame? We need to lean into warmth, appreciation, and self-compassion in our lives. We often get caught up in complaining about others and ourselves. We are not very practiced in noticing and expressing how we feel. Because we are naturally drawn to negative qualities, we stop noticing our good qualities. This becomes the wallpaper of our experience. Our mind can be unfair, believing if we work hard and are accomplished, we might like ourselves more.

What words do you use to describe yourself? Did you use accomplishments or was your description value based? Examples of value-based descriptions are: kind, honest, caring.

_____
_____
_____
_____
_____
_____
_____
_____
_____

"Overachievers have a tremendous feeling of self-doubt about their abilities coupled with a strong need to prove themselves." Robert Arkin

The Downside of Overachieving

An overachiever can often feel very lonely and distant from others in their relationships. The distance feels cold and can create a negative emotional space. Sadness, pain and anger can quickly snowball into anxiety and depression. At this point, the expert part is usually accompanied by the inner critic. This is the exact opposite intention of the expert part.

Feeling alone makes us feel imperfect or broken. Feeling imperfect makes overachievers push even harder to become better. The vicious cycle continues. Just like Carol's experience, it can lead to physical problems and/or drug and alcohol abuse. Overachievers alienate themselves from their authentic self. Ironically, all this is not the intent of the expert part. Many of the clients we work with don't even know what they're working towards, what their end goal is, or what their ideal life could look like.

Education Hangover

Our education hangover is essentially baggage from time spent trying to become an expert in many areas. When we were in school, we learned that education was a clear path to success. We grew up with a belief that knowledge and expertise would provide us with confidence and success in life. We truly love to learn, and often have to pause and ask ourselves, "Why take this course or sign up for that program?" Is it something we are truly interested in, or do we just need another certificate? When will we be good enough to do all the things that light us up? How many gold stars do we need?

Sobering up from our constant need to take courses and from our honour roll hangover is powerful. We have to become friends with our experts. The first step, as always, is self-awareness, noticing when we feel driven by other people's expectations or the belief that we are not enough.

'Self-security is the open and nonjudgmental acceptance of one's own weaknesses.' Alice Huang and Howard Berenbaum

Suzanne's Story

Look At Me, I Am Special

Another way for the expert to show up is to create opportunities to always stand out or to be seen. This is an example of how an expert part manifested in Suzanne. As the eldest of two with a brother with a developmental disability, many of my childhood memories are of my sibling and the care and attention he required. My parents were young and loved us both deeply. They, of course, struggled with their own wounds but always had the best of intentions, which I honour. I also simultaneously recognize that their best intentions did not always provide me with the attention I needed. Fifty some years ago, the trend was to shun people with developmental disabilities by placing them in residential facilities to only visit them occasionally. My parents, my mother especially, were pioneers in building an inclusive world where people with developmental disabilities could live a rich and full life in community. That, however, came with many challenges, as I remember us travelling from doctor to specialist to find help for my brother and my family. To my young self, there was only time and attention for him, and the message I received was to figure things out for myself because I was capable. It's interesting, even to this day, to hear my mother describe me as a baby and a child. She will say I was the perfect baby, I slept well, didn't cry much and was easy to care for.

One memory I have is of sitting in what I now know to be a case conference with many professionals in the room. I was 7 or 8; it was a large room, the chairs were covered in orange fabric (you know, that 70s look) with dark brown wooden arm rests. We had been there for what seemed to be a long time, and I remember being quite agitated, even though I was usually shy and reserved. I remember moving my arms side to side and thinking, "*If I keep moving, they will think there is something wrong or different with me, and they will ask me questions.*" It was an innocent thought at that moment; however, decades later, I realize how profound that was for my young self. It was a child desperately wanting to be seen and acknowledged. If they found something wrong or different about me, then I would get attention just like my brother.

By the way, they never did notice my agitation that day, and I traveled back into myself to sort it out alone. What did happen though is in this desire to be seen, acknowledged, and noticed, I spent a lifetime creating circumstances in my life where I stood out, from my choice of a post-secondary program, to the jobs I have held, to the red flashy linen suit I once owned (P.S. I still love that suit!).

I wondered several years ago why there was always a unique aspect to my jobs, and it occurred to me that it was a very subtle way of standing out and being seen without having to overtly be the centre of attention....always just enough for someone to say, "*She is the only one who does that. There are very few people who can do that. She is unique. She is an expert. I can't believe she has taken that course. Wow, look what she is doing.*" The truth is the part of me who created unique circumstances for most of my life was the 7 or 8-year-old girl in that large room with all those adults who just wanted someone to see her for who she was. Climbing the corporate ladder, having unique positions, or working on difficult projects or with vulnerable populations has created a lot of stress in my life. In recognizing this part of myself, I can now choose activities that light me up and feed my heart and soul rather than my need for external validation and recognition. I can tell that young girl in the orange chair how much I value her, and I can recognize how hard she is trying. As I hold her with compassion and tell her how truly special she is, she begins to soften, and I see the realization in her eyes that she no longer has to try so hard.

You don't have to be an expert. No one is expecting you to be an expert. All you need to do is show up and be you.

REALignment Practices

In the space below with your non-dominant hand draw a common household item without looking at the page. Some ideas: a bicycle, a teapot, or a lamp. Maybe even one of your pets! Though it may feel uncomfortable to do, you will likely be surprised at how interesting your sketch is despite it not being "perfect". Doing this practice regularly will help you let go of control and fear of failure and accept that expertise is non-existent. "Good enough" is better than never started, never done. Good enough might even be best.

_____
_____
_____
_____
_____
_____
_____

Make a list of those areas in your life where you feel a strong urge to be an expert. It could be at work, at home, or with extended family or friends. Choose one and examine why you have this need to be the expert. Was there something in your childhood that contributed to this need? In what way does it serve you now? In what way does it harm or burden you? The next time you feel the need to demonstrate your expertise in this area, see if you can notice the feeling and thank it for showing up but do not act on it.

_____
_____
_____
_____
_____
_____
_____
_____
_____

Draw or doodle your perfectionist and expert parts and name them.

Chapter 5

The Imposter Part in Me

"I still have a little imposter syndrome... It doesn't go away, that feeling that you shouldn't take me that seriously. What do I know? I share that with you because we all have doubts in our abilities, about our power and what that power is."— Michelle Obama

AS THE DEBATE OVER the underlying causes of imposter syndrome carries on, those who find themselves experiencing it can take heart in the fact that they're not alone. Everyone from Lady Gaga to Michelle Obama has reported feeling anxious about their qualifications from time to time. It's perfectly normal.

Have you ever heard a voice inside you whisper, *"You can't do that"* or *"Who do you think you are?"* Perhaps this has happened when you've been presented with an exciting, new or huge opportunity. A healthy dose of uncertainty about our skill set and education level can be a positive motivator. It helps us fill our toolbox with necessary tools to be credible and impactful. However, when we find ourselves signing up for endless workshops and courses, it might be a sign to pause and reflect on what is fueling our quest for credentials. Just like the perfection and expert parts, imposter parts are also members of our team of protectors who work hard to keep us from being exposed to uncomfortable feelings.

There is a reason why you can sometimes feel like a fraud despite having diplomas or important accomplishments. You have a part of you that is unconsciously afraid of your greatness, or has learned to play small. It is protecting you from judgment. In order to understand your impostor part, you need to befriend it, so it can work with you, instead of against you. Many of us have imposter feelings, which on occasion, make us feel that we are somehow fraudulent, despite the evidence that we are not. These feelings usually pass but sometimes the part can take over and play the leading role in some of our experiences. When this happens, we often self-sabotage or in other words deliberately hinder our own success in an attempt to confirm our thoughts and feelings. This stops us from achieving our full potential or engaging in what lights us up.

There is a connection between imposter feelings and our mental health. Due to repeated feelings of inadequacy, a person struggling with imposter feelings can develop other mental health conditions. For instance, negative feelings could lead to low motivation, anxiety, or depression. Other consequences associated with our imposter part include burnout, physical symptoms, and decreased job satisfaction and performance. Having an over-developed imposter part is a common phenomenon in western culture. A scroll through social media tells you all you need to know. We are taught to *"disrupt it," "beat it," or "avoid"* it with three easy steps. However, when we pause and reflect on what's beneath the surface of imposter feelings (worthlessness and shame), it is not possible to wave a magic wand as a relief strategy. We must befriend our imposter part!

Shame- Worth Another Mention

The imposter is rooted in shame. We have talked about shame in previous chapters, but it is worth another exploration in this chapter. Shame is pervasive and yes, we all experience it. It is considered one of the deepest emotions on the emotional scale. It is the belief that who we are at our very core is not good enough, or that we are unlovable and unworthy of connection. Humans are meant for connection, so when we believe that we are not worthy of connection it affects us so deeply. Many of us carry deep shame that we aren't even aware of until we begin paying attention to what we are feeling. Brené Brown describes shame as *"the fear of disconnection, the fear that something we have done or failed to do makes us unworthy of connection".*

Where Does It Come From?

The imposter part can emerge as a coping strategy for significant trauma. We also recognize that seemingly ordinary experiences can be traumatizing. The imposter part holds limiting beliefs and fear usually developed at a very early age. Our imposter is an adaptive pattern that helps us make sense of the world and feel safer within it. This part holds limiting beliefs and fears usually developed at an early age. The imposter part is the expert parts' internal twin. Although they have taken separate paths and created different results, their self-beliefs are the same. Significant people in our early years contribute to our self-beliefs and self-image. We learn what is valued and what gets approval or disapproval. Just like all our parts, the imposter part comes from our early life experiences. Do you have an idea about the origins of your imposter parts?

Let's take a moment to reflect on this. Use the space below to jot down what emerges:

_____
_____
_____
_____
_____
_____
_____
_____
_____
_____
_____
_____
_____

Jorge recalls a defining moment when they were in grade seven. They had a fear of the lab Bunsen burner and the open gas flame, and was hesitant and fearful to perform science experiments. During one experiment, Jorge's long-time school friend declared out loud in front of the class, that Jorge was dumb. The teacher didn't correct the other student or get curious about Jorge's fear. The teacher suggested with conviction that the student should prove their declaration. Jorge recalls shrinking back in the lab stool wishing that they were invisible. They were unable to speak. Perhaps this was when the seeds of doubt were planted and they internalized a belief that "I am not smart enough." "I am dumb." This is where Jorge's imposter part emerged.

When Wounds Surface

At the age of 48, Jorge's grade seven experience came to life with the belief "I am stupid." They were a manager bringing 20 years of knowledge and five years of leadership experience. They recall the impromptu meeting, the corner office and his face. There they were with a *'deer in the headlights'* look, as the supervisor asked a very simple question: *"What is your leadership style?"* Jorge's adult self could answer this question, hands down, with a long list of examples, confidence and grace. However, at that exact moment in time, they froze. Actually, Jorge's 12-year-old self, their imposter part, stood frozen in time. There was something about the supervisor's look, his eyes, his voice, his mannerism that triggered the grade seven experience. (Holy Hell- it felt like the Bunsen burner experience all over again!) Jorge opened their mouth and could not believe what they heard. It was a language nobody could understand. Jorge's words were slurred and made no sense. This is what happens when a wounded younger part, such as your imposter, takes the lead role in a situation.

Pause and Pivot

Jorge was able to notice that their imposter part was activated, and took a pause and a deep breath. That space gave Jorge an opportunity to pivot. In their mind's eye, Jorge hugged their 12-year-old self and thanked the imposter part for trying to protect them. Jorge's authentic self was able to confidently articulate their leadership style, strengths, and goals. Engaging in the pause and breathing creates the space for self-compassion and gives you an opportunity to pivot. This is the difference between reacting and responding.

Can you think of a time when your imposter part was the uninvited star of the show? Take a moment to reflect and record:

Imposter Party

Do not feel alone if this chapter is striking some nerves. As a clinical supervisor, Carmen witnesses, in general terms, a sense of not feeling good enough in many of the new therapists she supervises. Carmen deals a lot with graduate students who are qualifying to become registered psychotherapists. Sometimes they feel not good enough despite their education, hard work and knowledge. The imposter part is that persistent voice that says, "One day someone will find out I've been faking it!"

Recently, Carmen facilitated a clinical supervision group with 8 psychotherapists. The therapists were asked, "What activates your imposter part and how do you notice it?" Some situations that trigger their imposter parts are when the client wants the therapist to cure them or wants a quick fix; they work with a new issue; older clients with more life experience; or when clients put them on a pedestal. Some of the characteristics they notice within themselves when this part is activated are: a lack of internalizing success and achievements, discounting or minimizing success, guilt, fear about success, fear of failure, perfectionism, and undervaluing themselves. I know firsthand that they are brilliant, knowledgeable, caring and compassionate professionals. Imposter feelings are a typical occurrence. This part is trying to protect us, so let's get to know it.

Early in our careers, maintaining any professional role can sometimes feel like wearing a costume. Becoming a good therapist or professional starts with understanding our parts with compassion and dialing back our perfection, expert and imposter parts. This is true in any profession or role we play. It's only over the course of time that we return to real and show up authentically. As we discussed in the previous chapters, nobody can have a life free of struggles. If therapists did, we wouldn't be able to relate to our clients. Even the most successful professionals in the world are still human, with their own anxieties, fears, concerns and lived experiences. Even therapists who have been practicing for years sometimes experience this imposter feeling, us included.Fear of Failure

"I have written 11 books, but each time I think, Uh oh, they are going to find out now. I've run a game on everybody, and they're going to find me out." Maya Angelou

Our imposter parts are so afraid of failure and will do anything to avoid failing or of being 'found out' of their perceived failures. How incredibly exhausting it is to carry the belief that at any moment someone will discover that we are not as competent as people believe we are. We are fascinated by Maya Angelou's account of her imposter part. A Nobel Laureate with 11 published books was afraid of being found out. Fortunately for us, she never let her fear stop her from producing beautiful literature. So many of us do let our fear of failure and of being perceived as incompetent from pursuing our goals and dreams. What if we were able to work with our imposter part to help it to view failure with curiosity rather than with judgement? What if our notion of failure was transformed into the realization that as human beings, we experience a spectrum of emotions?

REAL Stories

In private practice, we often work with clients who doubt their skills. For example, they may have to lead a meeting or provide training, and do not feel like they know enough or that they are good enough or competent enough. They may feel that somebody is going to expose them to their incompetence. It is as if they have managed to get into a position where they feel they do not belong. This is such a common feeling for us too! Noticing your imposter part is an opportunity to learn and is a normal part of the cycle of growth.

We have worked with many adult children of alcoholics. We see clients who took the message of "*I am not good enough*" from childhood and said "*Let me show you I am worthy.*" This creates strong perfection, expert, and imposter parts. A significant portion of our clients have healthy self-worth but can still be plagued by self-doubt and imposter thoughts and feelings. These are symptoms of self-doubt and negative childhood messages. Let's take a closer look.

Sanjay, age 42, recalls how he felt after receiving his Doctor of Medicine: "*I worked so hard in medical school and I graduated top of my class. I have written many scientific research papers but I don't want my medical community to see how dumb they sound. I can't believe I have that degree. I wonder if my field is just really easy?"* Sanjay runs a medical unit and is parenting three young children. Deep down, he knew he was doing it all, but the nagging self-doubt kept him from giving himself credit.

Trish, a mother of two, and a college professor, started on her journey to return to real. She reports that she is unable to give herself credit for anything she achieves. She carried deep inside her, an old belief, that she cannot measure up to anybody. Her personal rat race of chasing more and more titles and achievements did not provide her with self-worth or a sense of *"I am enough."* Her imposter part would not allow her to take credit for any of her accomplishments.

If you are a high achiever chasing your chosen life passions, giving yourself credit while taking care of yourself, you are on the right track. The imposter part becomes a problem when you cannot give yourself credit for what you accomplish in your life. This can manifest as mental, emotional, or physical issues associated with not taking care of yourself. Also, if you only seek external validation to define your self-worth, your imposter part will never feel satisfied.

Have you dismissed outward signs of accomplishments as just luck or good timing? Do you play down your positive attributes? This is the power of internalized messages. Take a moment to reflect and write down anything that comes up for you.

Many incredibly competent women and men have shared similar stories. If you have accomplishments and have worked hard, it is real. You can give yourself credit!

"People are like stained-glass windows. They sparkle and shine when the sun is out, but when the darkness sets in, their true beauty is revealed only if there is a light from within." Elizabeth Kubler-Ross

Compassion Is Our Best Friend

For anyone experiencing the imposter part, instead of trying to banish your imposter parts (it just doesn't work), befriend them. Get to know this part and hear its story. As always, compassion is our best friend when getting to know a part of ourselves. By admitting that we have experienced imposter feelings, we give ourselves permission to get to know it with kindness. Compassion cultivates a growth mindset and is our best way to overcome the sense that we are not good enough.

You will learn that your imposter part has been trying to keep you safe from humiliation and that its intention is pure. Are you willing to offer compassion to a part that has been trying to keep you safe? Eventually, you will learn why your part adopted this protective strategy. You might start to feel the weighted feeling of worthlessness, when your part is fully witnessed. It's normal and perfectly healthy to sit with your discomfort for a few minutes. Eventually, with time and practice (doing the REALignment practices), your imposter part will soften. Your true authentic self has the power to compassionately dial back this part, so you can lean into your authenticity. This internal shift is a sign of a growth mindset, a belief that we can learn and improve with practice.

Kindly Dial Back Your Imposter Part

Attempts to control our parts worsen their grip on us. All our parts soften with self-compassion and this shift creates psychological flexibility, or what we like to call pause and pivot. Imagine holding this imposter part in your hand, up close to your eyes. When we are entangled in our thoughts, we hold them so close. When we are this close to it, we cannot see it. We ask that you hold your hand out in front of your body at arm's length. Create some space between your hand and your body. Now examine this part from a distance. Does it feel different? Are you able to see this part differently? Can you understand why it is trying to help you? This perspective shift can help you see the imposter as a part. It is not you. It is a part of you. You can distance yourself compassionately and dial back the intensity by creating the space.

"I still sometimes feel like a loser kid in high school and I just have to pick myself up and tell myself that I'm a superstar

every morning so that I can get through this day and be for my fans what they need for me to be."— Lady Gaga

Permission To Play Big

The bigger you play, the more likely you are going to be criticized. We find great comfort and inspiration in a favourite passage by Marianne Williamson, and hope you will too.

"Our deepest fear is not that we are inadequate. Our deepest fear is that we are powerful beyond measure. It is our light, not our darkness that most frightens us. We ask ourselves, 'Who am I to be brilliant, gorgeous, talented, fabulous?' Actually, who are you not to be? You are a child of God. Your playing small does not serve the world. There is nothing enlightened about shrinking so that other people won't feel insecure around you. We are all meant to shine, as children do. We were born to manifest the glory of God that is within us. It's not just in some of us; it's in everyone. And as we let our own light shine, we unconsciously give other people permission to do the same. As we are liberated from our own fear, our presence automatically liberates others." Marianne Williamson

REALignment Practices

Find a comfortable seated or lying position, close your eyes, and take a few deep breaths. Invite your imposter part into your attention. If it is helpful, hold out your hand away from your body and invite your imposter to rest there. Listen to what your imposter part is saying about trying to keep you safe. Try to hold this with compassion and understanding for up to 30 seconds. If this feels too difficult, start with 10 seconds. Notice how it feels in your body when you hold compassion for your imposter part.

Return to this practice as often as needed and work up to holding compassion and understanding for your imposter part up to several minutes at a time.

In this space, write down 20 accomplishments that you have achieved in your lifetime. Everything counts. Nothing is too small or insignificant. Once you've written down 10, try to squeeze out 5 more (or as many as are available to you). Keep this list of accomplishments in a place where you can refer back to it often. Add new accomplishments to this list as they happen and take a moment to reflect on what you've achieved each time you do. Bonus points if you find a small way to celebrate each time you add an accomplishment.

Practice the pause and pivot (stop and shift) in low-risk situations. When you feel your imposter rising mentally give yourself a hug, take a breath, and thank your imposter for trying to protect you. To begin with, practice this when you are alone and you notice your imposter rising in your thoughts. The more you practice, the more you will begin to notice that the pause and pivot become your automatic response whenever the imposter arises, and that you will be able to call upon it for more challenging situations.

Draw or doodle your imposter part and name it.

Chapter 6

The Rescuer Part in Me

"Help will come, but help is not rescuing. We are our own rescuers. Our relationships will improve dramatically when we stop rescuing others and stop expecting them to rescue us."
Melody Beattie

To help others is a beautiful demonstration of our humanity and we want to encourage that kindness, that sense of altruism in you. In fact, there is evidence that extending ourselves and helping others leads to greater happiness and fulfillment in life. Please continue to volunteer at your child's school or in your community, bake muffins for a fundraiser or sit with an elderly person, if that is what lights you up. This is what makes our world a better place. These acts of helpfulness and kindness are not what we are talking about in this chapter.

In this chapter we are delving into the rescuer subpersonality. This is the part of us that believes it is our job to save others from themselves. The part that believes we can fix others. It becomes problematic when it dominates our life or drives the bus of our life. You may recognize this in yourself or perhaps have known people who seem to gravitate towards very needy people. When the rescuer part is activated, you may notice a sense of micro-managing others' lives and making decisions for them, believing that they are incapable of making their own choices or decisions. This can be quite exhausting and damaging, especially in intimate partner relationships. The rescuer personality is often hyper-focused on others rather than on their own inner world. Their lives can revolve around others - they exist to save others from themselves. The rescuer personality will often insert themselves into the lives of others as a means of increasing their value and their sense of worth. They learned, likely very early on, that they were valued and loved as a helper.

Let's get to know this inner part which is holding us prisoner. When there is unpredictability or chaos, children often survive by becoming 'the adult' at an early age. Consequently, they know very little about play and what lights them up. In psychological terms, we say children were 'parentified', meaning in order to ensure their own emotional or psychological survival they became the parent, the caretaker, the reasonable one, the responsible one. These children are often characterized and praised as 'so mature for their age and so responsible'. In truth, they are being robbed of their childhood and the experience of seeing the world through the eyes of innocence.

Again, this chapter is not about blaming or shaming parents. We wholeheartedly believe that people and parents do the best they can. The challenge for most humans is not how to avoid suffering because that is impossible. The challenge is how to sit with pain that is inherent in our lives, and how not to create more suffering by our attempts to numb, avoid or distract from pain. Children raised in chaos or unpredictability have families in which physical and psychological safety was not always present. They adapt to their environment by developing several parts, such as the victim or the rescuer.

Imagine the burden of that responsibility as a child. Imagine trying to be a good little girl or boy so that maybe your parents will notice you, connect with you, or love you. What if being a little helper actually improved your life? It makes sense at the moment, however, there is no time to be a carefree, fun-loving child, as there is often worry about what will happen next and what they need to do. These children also often know very little about boundaries as there is an enmeshing or entanglement of emotion and identity. This can be triggering. If you experience discomfort as you read this, pause and be kind to yourself.

When a child is raised in a healthy environment, they learn that they have a capable parent who is taking care of them. They learn to trust that their well-being is being looked after and are able to differentiate between their role and that of their parents. Children who experience an unpredictable childhood may grow up to be adults who don't know where their responsibilities begin and end because a parent was never able to model that behaviour for them. There can be little awareness of boundaries and they may find themselves performing duties that others can easily do for themselves or taking on other responsibilities.

"Boundaries are the relational lines that determine what's okay and what's not okay in our interactions and relationships with ourselves and others." Brené Brown

Brené also says "Boundaries are the distance at which I can love you and me simultaneously."

With an active rescuer subpersonality, there is no loving you and me simultaneously because there are little to no boundaries, and there is little to no awareness of where you end and the other begins. The rescuer can be an in-your-face type of person, one that can quite easily take over for another. Children who adapt by taking on a rescuer subpersonality tend to develop a codependent role in future relationships and they become adults who only know the burden of helping others, while numbing their own needs.

Does any of this seem familiar to you? Let's take a moment to reflect on this. Use the space below to jot down what emerges:

_____
_____
_____
_____
_____
_____
_____
_____
_____
_____
_____
_____

Codependency

Much has been written on codependency as a psychological concept and an entire chapter could have been dedicated to exploring this notion. We wanted to include this topic in this particular chapter because of the link between the rescuer part of ourselves and that of codependency. It is often recognized as a relationship dynamic associated with addictions, but it also applies to exposure to other childhood traumas or experiences.

Codependency, in simple terms, refers to people who feel extreme amounts of dependence on certain loved ones in their lives, and who feel responsible for the feelings and actions of those loved ones. Codependency can be characterized as the excessive sense of responsibility for the other's wellbeing and the imbalance between giving and receiving and providing support as well as several other attributes. Those with rescuer tendencies can be powerful enablers.

Codependency in the rescuer personality can manifest in several ways. They often experience low self esteem and may be extremely loyal to others continuing to do things which may be harmful to themselves. They may take on the feelings of others and can be hypervigilant about others' feelings.

This is what it can look like:

- Having difficulty identifying what you are feeling.
- Minimizing, altering, or denying how you truly feel.
- Perceiving yourself as completely unselfish and dedicated to the wellbeing of others.
- Believing you can take care of yourself without any help from others.
- Masking pain in various ways such as with anger, humour, or isolation.

There may also be a belief with this personality type that others are incapable of taking care of themselves hence the drive to rescue and take care of them.

We all have loved ones we feel a sense of responsibility towards and want to help, however, the challenge arises when we take on that sense of responsibility or duty at the detriment of our own wellbeing. It is an unhealthy pattern when our self-worth is attached to the need to rescue someone or to take responsibility for them.

The Wounded Healer

As mentioned in the first chapter, sensitive or wounded people may be drawn to work in a helping profession. A wounded healer is a deeply empathic person who cares deeply for others. Problems develop when the helping professional cannot distinguish between their personal issues and those they are supporting. This is why it is of utmost importance for helping professionals to befriend their rescue-part and heal their wounds. Once healed, they develop a deeper attunement with others who have suffered.

Nobody escapes being wounded. We are all wounded people, whether physically, emotionally, mentally, or spiritually. The main question is not, *"How can we hide our wounds so we don't have to be embarrassed?"* but *"How can we align our woundedness with supporting others?"*

"When our wounds cease to be a source of shame, and become a source of healing, we have become wounded healers." – Henri Nouwen

When Helpers Allow the Rescue Part to Take the Lead

A common characteristic of the rescuer is that the helper does for the other, instead of believing in the other person's internal process for healing. The rescuer takes on the problem of the other and does its best to fix them or protect them from anything that might cause distress or pain. For example, new therapists often feel the urge to have all the solutions and to show up to lead clients from despair to relief. The rescue part will go to extraordinary lengths, such as returning phone calls and emails at all hours of the day and night. In therapy, we might refer to this as poor boundaries and it results in dependence on the therapist. As we become more experienced (and heal our own wounds), we start to give ourselves permission to not have all the answers. This is a freeing awareness which allows the rescue part to relax, and our real self leads the sessions.

We embrace Dr. Gabor Maté's description of the compassion of possibility, the fifth and most difficult level of compassion, as he describes. It is the ability to see people for their possibilities and potential rather than the way in which they show up. This concept has changed the way we see clients and the way we behave as parents. As self-declared rescuers, it is no mystery that we chose this type of career. We started our careers believing we would change the world. This is not uncommon amongst mental health and health care professionals. It is exhausting though and extremely limiting for the client or patient. The compassion of possibility speaks to recognizing that while the person sitting in front of you identifies with their dysfunctions and impairments (that's why they have sought your help) we, as practitioners, can choose to see them for their possibilities, for the real self under the dysfunction or problem. If we believe (and we do) that our core being is simply covered up by these coping mechanisms we had to create as an adaptation to our environment, then imagine what it must feel like to experience someone seeing you for who you truly are, in all your wisdom, in all of your possibilities.

What if we practiced compassion of possibility as a parent, as a partner, as a daughter, as a son, as an employee, as a citizen of our world. Our own experience as parents has changed since beginning to practice this. Where we used to want to immediately jump in and rescue our children, even as adults, at any opportunity because we did not believe they were capable of resolving issues on their own, we can now take a step back and watch them, often with great joy, discovering their potential and their truths. Let's be honest, it is gut-wrenching at times witnessing their pain when they encounter difficult times and we are often tempted to jump into the turbulent waters with them. That moment of pause and acknowledgement of the rescuer part, however, provides an opportunity to remember that they have their own competencies, abilities and innate wisdom. We will, of course, help them should they need, but for now we have the freedom to stand on the sidelines and witness them walking their path.

Relationships and the Rescuer

In relationships our rescue part finds it hard to receive. It is more comfortable giving or even self-sacrificing. When this part is playing the lead role in life, there is a possibility that we are in relationships with selfish or narcissistic partners. You might fantasize about receiving, but continue to give and give. It's a symptom and becomes an obstacle to receiving real love. We are rescuing others and forgetting about our wants, needs and desires.

Let's take a moment to pause and reflect on the times when you neglected your own needs and how that felt. Use the space below to record what emerges:

_____
_____
_____
_____
_____
_____
_____
_____
_____
_____
_____
_____

Receiving What We Give

When your wounds feel raw, unresolved, and exposed, it doesn't mean you have to rescue the world. This desire to rescue may be a distraction from your personal inner pain. Giving is not the answer. Receiving compassion and kindness is paramount. Self-compassion guides us to get to know our rescue part without judgment. This is your healing journey and it is important to create space each day to practice self-compassion. According to Dr. Kristin Neff, there are three elements of practicing self-compassion: self-kindness versus self-judgment, common humanity versus isolation, and mindfulness versus over-identification. These guiding principles can help us interact with our rescue part in a new and healing way. We encourage you to apply these principles of self-compassion. Listen with empathy and compassion as you imagine this part of you.

Sometimes when we hang our professional hats for a day, we have a tendency to review the memories of some of the day's stressors. Did I miss something? Did I do enough? What can I do differently? This worry and questioning will dry our well of compassion to the point where compassion fatigue may set in. This is a signal that our rescue part is activated or playing the leading role. This is another opportunity to pause and pivot.

Being a parent continues to teach us how to heal our own rescue part. When we notice this part, we pause and sit with the emotions with compassion and kindness (raw) and in this magical pause we notice a decrease in intensity. This allows us to pivot and choose a different response, a new practice (risky). It is easy to just keep plowing through with support, advice, and directions when obstacles come up for the people we love. While the *"harder I try, the better I do"* thought process used to work, it no longer does. Sometimes, you just need to take a breath and pause, look closely at the situation and subpersonality, and then decide whether it is best to keep helping, pushing or to pivot in another direction. If you always do what you have always done, you will always experience the same result. Letting people walk in their own life lessons and trusting that they have the answers within themselves, can be very freeing.

As we commit over and over again to pausing and leaning into our feelings (raw), and engage new actions to pivot (risky), we rediscover our authentic self (real). Our personal journey ripples outwards to others and triggers their own healing journey.

Yasmin's story

Yasmin knew the rescuer part of her personality very well. It was born out of having a sister with a developmental disability. The words of her well-intentioned parents were well ingrained. At the tender age of 7, her sister would have been 6 and about to start school. Her mother explained that Yasmin's role was to take care of her sister while they were in school. Yasmin's interpretation of her mother's message was that it was her sole responsibility to take care of her younger sister. She recalls the conversation; the fear and worry in her mother's voice as she was about to release her vulnerable little girl into the world without her protection. The seriousness and heaviness Yasmin felt from that conversation created an imprint which has guided her life. It impacted her choice of career and her relationships. As a child, she worried constantly about what needed to be done next to take care of her family. She was not a carefree, fun-loving child. There was always something to worry about and to plan for.

As a young adult, she was always the one in-charge of making decisions, ensuring everyone was safe, fed, and comfortable. In her mind that kept them safe. She developed into a very capable adult, accomplishing almost everything she set out to do. This part of herself made her an incredible planner and a very efficient worker because there always seemed to be so much to do. Rescuing people is a full-time job, on top of everything else that needs to be done. After engaging in therapy, she is now able to acknowledge the positive traits of this part of herself, as well those exhausting traits which no longer serve her. The latter are the ones she is learning to release. The more aware she becomes of this part of herself, the better she recognizes the competence and potential in others. This reduces the need to rescue, allowing others the freedom of their journey. Yasmin no longer needs others to be ok to be ok herself. How freeing is that!

REALignment Practices

In this space, make two columns. In the first, write down 10 ways that you neglect your own needs. Now think of 10 counter-actions - one for each neglect - you can put into practice to nurture your own needs and put these in the second column. Use the second column as your go-to self-care list when you feel depleted.

Do you subscribe to "the harder I try the better I do philosophy"? If yes, reflect on how it's working for you. How does it make you feel emotionally, physically, and mentally? Reflect on whether subscribing to this philosophy served you at a different time in your life. Often, when we are younger and have fewer responsibilities working as hard as we can as much as we can nets positive results. As we get older and our responsibilities shift there is often less energy to give to meeting every demand that comes our way. Ask if there is a way to be kinder to yourself in how you approach tasks and expectations. Try these affirmations to help you - tape them to your mirror or add them as daily reminders on your phone:

- It's okay for things to feel easy.

- It's safe for me to take care of my own needs, even if it means disappointing others.

- My needs are just as important as the needs of others.

- There's a kinder way of approaching this and I'm open to trying it.

- Whatever I do, I see as being enough.

Chapter 7

The Victim Part in Me

"Your conflicts, all the difficult things, the problematic situations in your life are not chance or haphazard. They are actually yours. They are specifically yours, designed specifically for you by a part of you that loves you more than anything else. The part of you that loves you more than anything else has created roadblocks to lead you to yourself. You are not going in the right direction unless there is something pricking you in the side, telling you, "Look here! This way!" That part of you loves you so much that it doesn't want you to lose the chance. It will go to extreme measures to wake you up, it will make you suffer greatly if you don't listen. What else can it do? That is its purpose." A. H Almaas

MANY SUBPERSONALITIES CAN EMERGE throughout our lifetime. As we have mentioned in almost every chapter there is always a good reason for the creation of these parts within ourselves. Let's remember that all behaviours are adaptive and that at some point in our lives they were likely essential to our psychological safety and wellbeing. These subpersonalities that we create to adapt to our environment serve us well, until they no longer serve us. In our quest towards a return to real we intentionally focused on subpersonalities we see in our professional lives most often. Some of these subpersonalities we also identify with, to some degree.

It is important to recognize that we may relate to some of these traits to varying degrees in different areas of our lives. As an example, while victimhood may not be a dominant trait, we may have moments in our lives where we experience a sense of being a victim. There are often areas of our lives where we tend to take on a victim role more easily. We mention this so that you can recognize that these personality traits can live on a spectrum.

The victim part is a difficult one to talk about and it may be easily misinterpreted and can appear to minimize one's difficult experiences and suffering. Let's be clear about a few things. We believe:

- What happened to you as a child was NOT your fault. You were a victim of whatever happened to you.

- You do not need to have experienced a traumatic event to experience trauma. Let's remember that we align with the definition that trauma is not what happened to you, it is how you interpret what happened.

- Adults can be victims of many unfortunate circumstances.

Not everyone who has experienced trauma or has been victimized will develop a victim subpersonality, just as everyone who has experienced trauma will develop perfectionist or rescuer tendencies.

The World is Out to Get Me

Many of us have been victimized in childhood and as adults. As such we can become overly identified with victimhood, believing that our life is completely outside of our control and under the control of luck, fate or others. Have you ever heard yourself or someone say something like, 'this is just my luck" or "if something bad is going to happen, it will happen to me." These are indications that you may identify with a victim mindset.

"You're only a victim to the degree of what your perception allows." - Shannon L. Alder

Those with a victim tendency may see the world as a dangerous and unkind place to live, believing that life is conspiring against them. There is often a tendency to 'catastrophize' situations and to engage in negative self-talk. How else could this subpersonality survive without negativity and drama? The reality is bad things happen to everyone; however, this is not easily recognized by those with a victim mindset, believing they have a target on their back.

The victim part can show up as avoidance from taking responsibility for your decisions, actions, choices and your life. Those with this mindset have difficulty recognizing that they have any role at all in relationships and outcomes in their lives. They can feel paralyzed and unable to move out of their comfort zone or make any changes which could improve their life. This is a painful place to be, however as we've learned in the previous chapters it is a strategy to protect oneself from any more pain. What our parts don't know is that their attempts to protect us from pain, at some point in our lives will create even more pain.

"Staying with a negative experience past the point that's useful is like running laps in Hell: You dig the track a little deeper in your brain each time you go around it." Dr Rick Hanson

This mindset is often grounded in a sense of lack, particularly the lack of fairness. This part often feels like they do not have the same opportunities as others and have been treated unfairly and fail to recognize the role they play in the situation. Let us qualify this statement by stating that we wholeheartedly recognize and believe that systemic racism has denied many people and cultures of opportunities and even basic needs. We believe that white privilege exists. People across the world have been victims of systemic racism and of white privilege.

When we refer to the victim mindset and the sense of being treated unfairly, we speak of it from the point of view of an individual's coping strategy to mitigate hurt. Many people with a victim mindset and those with a dominant rescuer personality often believe they are martyrs. This can be a very destructive way of thinking.

"The victim mentality will have you dancing with the devil, then complaining that you're in hell." Steve Maraboli

Challenging our Limiting Beliefs

"I am not a victim. No matter what I have been through, I'm still here. I have a history of victory."- Steve Maraboli

We are not negating inexcusable, traumatizing experiences. The victim part we are discussing doesn't refer to these situations where you were truly a victim. This pattern refers to the situation where a part of you is attached to feeling like a victim, even when you are in a situation where you could now take steps to improve your situation. You should never ignore your past hurts and pain. Equally important is focusing on moving forward. It is important to focus on moving forward with what we can control, rather than living as a victim. Is it easy? No. Is it worth it? Yes. In other words, while what happened to you as a child was not your fault, as an adult, you have the responsibility to heal yourself.

"You are not a victim. No matter what you have been through, you're still here. You may have been challenged, hurt, betrayed, beaten, and discouraged, but nothing has defeated you. You are still here! You have been delayed but not denied. You are not a victim, you are a victor. You have a history of victory." Dr. Steve Maraboli

Seeing yourself as the victim feels natural if you have been harmed, treated poorly, or suffered at the hands of another. Experiencing trauma can shatter our assumptions that the world is a kind and generous place and make us believe that we are at the mercy of our fellow human beings. Rationally, it makes total sense to feel like a victim if your partner cheated, lied, was a card-carrying narcissist, or an insufferably contemptible (or all of the above). But, sadly, labeling and identifying yourself as a victim strips you of your power and piles pain on pain. Your victim part may feel very justified, but this justification also keeps it stuck..

You may have endured horrible pain. Maybe, you still are. But, stay with us here; seeing yourself as a victim of your experiences keeps you passive and stuck. You may feel as helpless as a starfish washed up on shore. You may have landed there, but you don't have to stay there.

It's much more empowering to know your victim part which is merely trying to protect you from feeling intense pain and the idea of being hurt again. Hiding underneath this part, is a purposeful person who can step up to make powerful choices. As in, you made (or are making) the choice to let go of your partner because they're not good for you, and you deserve better. Or you decide that you deserve more than staying in that toxic work environment.

This in no way negates the pain, sadness, and anger that comes with divorce and/or leaving that secure job. You need to acknowledge and give yourself time to process. It's truly about thanking your victim part for protecting you and then deciding not to cast yourself as a powerless victim. Although you may not like or immediately accept the choices in front of you, you do have choices.

Our Victim Part Keeps Us Stuck

The victim part focuses your energy on the other person, the job, religion, politics, and the world in general and not on truly recovering and healing. This is where many people get stuck. As an example of this, Bob left his partner to marry another with whom he had been having an affair. Ten years post-divorce, his ex-wife Janet was still very bitter. Janet had not moved on emotionally because she thought that releasing her anger was approving of the ex-partners' choices.

True or not, by holding on to her victim status, Janet was holding her own life hostage.

When the victim part of self is playing the lead role in life, it is a way to avoid fully facing and processing grief. For example, keeping the focus on the ex and what they did or didn't do is a way to keep pain at a manageable constant, sometimes for years or even a lifetime if you're not careful. Putting your attention on befriending your victim part and moving through your pain is healing yourself. This is a power move that takes grit, courage, and vulnerability.

The Victim Part Blames, Our Real Self Owns

There's another danger in playing the victim. When we are swallowed up in regret it can feel extremely heavy. It feels like a veritable ton of bricks on your back. Regret gives us an opportunity to dig deep and self-reflect. Maybe it's not something you did, but something you allowed.

"When you think everything is someone else's fault you suffer a lot. When you realize everything springs only from yourself, you will learn both peace and joy." Dalai Lama

How to Know if You're Trapped in the Victim Part

- You tend to blame others for your past or current circumstances.

- You can't identify any ways that you may have contributed to or participated in the unwanted results.

- You believe everything wrong was out of your control.

- You're invested in being "wronged" to the point that you think moving on and creating a better life will make the other person right.

- On some level, it's working for you to stay powerless because of the sympathy and commiseration you're getting, or it's too scary to move on for some other reason.

If one or more of these sounds uncomfortably familiar, ask yourself, "*Am I willing to trade feeling like a victim for feeling and exercising my own power over my life?*" Be honest. If the answer is, "Yes!" do what you need to do to heal and recover. When we realize that we are not defined by what happened in the past, we give ourselves permission to start talking about dreams and goals and the steps we could take to heal and move forward. If your victim part is saying, "No *way!*" or "Not *yet*," that's OK. Consider working with a therapist to help you process your feelings. If you are ready, let's dig a little deeper.

Does any of this seem familiar to you? Let's take a moment to reflect on this. Use the space below to jot down or draw what emerges:

Digging Deeper

The victim part is often associated with a childhood experience of not feeling seen and accepted, coming to believe that something is wrong with you. This part is formed to attract some affection from those who would otherwise not be paying attention. Sometimes we tend to see ourselves as being wronged by people or being in an impossible situation. Or we may have learned that we had to be sick or needy in order to receive attention and connection from others. *"Maybe this way I get some of the love and attention that I deserve."* Perhaps you believe that sadness is noble and shows exceptional depth, insight, and sensitivity. Are there times when you feel emotional and temperamental as a way to gain affection?

Record anything that may be rumbling around inside.

_____
_____
_____
_____
_____
_____
_____
_____
_____
_____
_____
_____
_____

You may feel like the victim of your circumstances, genetics and biology. You also may feel that there is nothing you can do about it. Powerless. When this part plays the lead role in your life, you find yourself thinking about how others have wronged or hurt you. When you are criticized you tend to withdraw, pout and sulk. You can be dramatic or create chaos in order to be seen. Perhaps when life becomes difficult, you want to crumble and give up. Repressed anger manifests as apathy, depression, and constant fatigue.

We often witness the rationalizations and the stories people make about why they cannot get their lives together. People often feel cheated and helpless about their life situations. You may make excuses to yourself about why you do not feel happy or fulfilled and feel cheated and helpless to do anything about it.

The victim part can keep us from setting intentions and goals for personal and professional development. This part interferes with our ability to change with purpose and determination. The trap of focussing on how other people are to blame for what has transpired in our life rather than believing we can create change can be debilitating. Some of the thought patterns might be *"no one understands me," "poor me,"* or *"bad things always happen to me."* There is usually a deep wish that someone will rescue you. Your need to be rescued may position you to attract people with a dominant rescuer personality. Remembering back to chapter 6 where we explored the rescuer personality, we know that the rescuer has a tendency for codependency, so if you meet your rescuer, you can be sure that he or she will perpetuate your victimhood. This is the perfect relationship storm.

"You are responsible for your life. You can't keep blaming others for your dysfunctions. Life is really about moving on." Oprah Winfrey

Impact on Others

This subpersonality's efforts often backfire by pushing people away. Others may feel frustrated, helpless, or guilty by this behaviour. They might feel like they are putting band-aids on your pain. On a deep level, this part is worried that you will lose your attachment if you become healthy.

Always with subpersonalities, a heightened awareness of the part and its tendencies can propel us into growth.

Difficult Terrain

We have explored very sensitive territory in this chapter. It is important to examine all our parts, and the dance they do together, as we listen to the music of our souls. When Carmen thinks of her wounds, the expert and perfectionist parts in her rise to defend the spaces and places she feels vulnerable. When that doesn't work, it's a slippery slope to victimhood, as her victim subpersonality takes over.

Carmen's Story

Throughout my life, my rescuer and perfectionist parts often took the lead in difficult situations, to defend those spaces and places I felt vulnerable. Then, I would beat myself up for being vulnerable, and needing to defend myself. It was a vicious circle.

Fast forward to the present and the word victim becomes a trigger for me. It was difficult to write this chapter and I now realize it's a familiar conversation and dance within me. When my rescue and perfection parts do not solve problems, feelings of failure and victim emerge. There is familiarity in the sensory cues in my body. Have you noticed sometimes when you are being vulnerable you hear something that causes your body to constrict? Sometimes it's very subtle, sometimes it is strong. When this happens, I tend to freeze, not physically, but intellectually. I have no words and I usually retreat to some age where I don't have the capacity to express what I'm feeling. I don't know what to do. This is what can happen to me when I witness someone I love, myself, or a client leaning into the victim wounds.

It takes me a few hours, or sometimes a few days, to sort through what happened. I now recognize when a constriction takes place, my victim part is driving the bus. Constriction is a by-product of my rescue part feeling stuck. The abort button is pushed, and it limits my potential to engage action and be real.

Choose growth over collapse and victim.

When we are aware of the subtle cues presenting in our body, we become aware of the invitation to notice which subpersonality is playing the lead role in the situation. In order to engage the invitation all we need to ask is, "Am I willing to relax into what is happening?" This is not the same as trying to intellectually understand a problem. It is more about describing the sensations e.g. "I feel a collapse taking place inside and what I desire is action." This can be a very difficult moment. Let go of the rational story and go beyond the judgement. This is not something we are taught, and it takes practice. I have over 25 years of providing therapy and I can still get caught in old dance steps of defending and protecting. Remember, it's about the journey, not the destination.

The Invitations

The words vulnerability and victim invite me into spaces and places I didn't know existed inside me. To discover something I didn't know before. My old dance steps include some form of a brilliant strategy with another part that's been playing out for years. Our parts' response is so woven into the fabric of our makeup, we don't recognize the part, or see the pattern. As in my personal experience, my rescue and perfection parts took over to hide the shame of my wounded younger victim part.

When the victim surfaces, my thoughts often go to, "*Why aren't they doing something about this. Get over it already.*" It's difficult in these moments for me to ask "*What is this moment inviting me to notice about myself. What is the big reveal within me?*" Imagine for a moment, when we look to blame others, that the situation becomes the invitation for us to discover something about ourselves.

If we recognize these moments as the invitations of reflection, and we offer compassion to our victim part, we notice a break in the pattern or dance steps.

Relating to my parts with compassion is what this human experience is for me. We are in a dance with our parts, the *"we in me."* How do we break the patterns that are so ingrained, we no longer see them as parts. It takes practice. What I do know is, it takes compassionate curiosity to invite an exploration for us to become more than what we believe we are. It's about staying in the tough conversations and daily reflections. As difficult as it is, it's our gateway to becoming real!

Let's take a moment to reflect on this. Use the space below to record what emerges:

When in your life has the victim part of you been more dominant?

What surprised you about what you have read so far in this chapter? How do you relate it to your life currently?

_____
_____
_____
_____
_____
_____
_____
_____
_____
_____
_____

Pulling Your Own Strings

In his book *Pulling Your Own Strings*, Dr. Wayne Dyer speaks of shifting out of a victim mindset by exercising our right to own our freedom and to choose the life we want to live.

If you have a victim mindset, recognize that you have a choice in how you want your life to be. It can be very difficult to even contemplate as it may seem so foreign to you.

In working with the victim subpersonality as with other personality traits it is so important to first and foremost recognize and acknowledge this as a part of the self. Begin to understand the purpose of that part of yourself and how it truly did protect you. How does it still protect you today? Sit with that for a moment. As always, extend compassion to yourself for your innate wisdom and begin to imagine the life you would choose for yourself.

"When you choose to act on your problems, you cease to be a victim of circumstance and become a force of change; that's when you transition to not only being a survivor, but to being a leader or hero too, and an inspiration to those still in the victim's mindset." – Innocent Mwatsikesimbe

REALignment Practices

Reflect on the statements 'this is just my luck' and 'if something bad is going to happen, it will happen to me.' Do you identify with these statements? Are they something you think or say often? The next time you notice yourself thinking or saying something similar, explore if it's really true. Are you really *always* unlucky? Do bad things *always* happen to you? Do things *never* go your way? When we begin to examine the absolutes behind those statements, we can start to de-identify with our victim part.

In this space, write down three lucky or positive things that happened in your life this past week. Then, try incorporating this exercise into your daily routine and notice how it affects you over time. Our brains are hardwired to focus on negative experiences and intentionally noticing positive things will train our brain to focus on the positive.

The next time a challenging situation arises try to take action rather than simply thinking about it. Decide on the next small, easy step you can take to make to improve the situation. Make sure this is an action you can take, not just a thought. Once you have decided on the step, take the action immediately. Notice how your body feels after you have taken the action. Record what you notice.

Chapter 8

Returning to Real Acceptance of the We in Me

"Owning our story and loving ourselves through that process is the bravest thing that we'll ever do." Brené Brown

CONGRATULATIONS! YOU HAVE ARRIVED at the final chapter. If you skipped ahead, we applaud your eagerness and invite you to flip back to some of the previous chapters to see what emerges for you. We recognize and acknowledge that irrespective of how long it has taken you to get here, you have no doubt experienced some difficult and reflective moments as you embarked on this journey with us.

Will the REAL You Come Forward?

Healing our wounds is not a quick, glamorous, or easy path. But it is the true path to healing and transformation. It is a journey! The return to real doesn't end here, in fact this is the beginning of the rest of your life with eyes and heart open. Each and every one of us is beautiful in our own right. You are on the path to becoming the free, unique, and beloved person you were created to be. This is the place where possibility lives and we cannot speak of a return to real without first having explored parts of ourselves. That was the purpose of chapters 2 to 7. The freedom to fully express ourselves, being our authentic selves, comes from the awareness of who we are right now.

We have written this book during a very difficult 2-year period; a global pandemic, unprecedented political unrest, a climate crisis, and many other complex world issues. We are noticing the heaviness of conflict and of the unknown. We believe that focusing on our own micro-healing and noticing our patterns in our daily roles as wife, partner, parent, friend, therapist, worker, neighbour, global citizen have far-reaching effects on the world. We regularly ask ourselves *"what energy am I contributing to humankind?"*

We ask ourselves *"what can we do?"* At the core of our healing, our greatest power is in healing our inner parts. Through this work, we create a better world for ourselves, our families, and our children.

"True belonging is the spiritual practice of believing in and belonging to yourself so deeply that you can share your most authentic self with the world and find sacredness in both being a part of something and standing alone in the wilderness. True belonging doesn't require you to change who you are; it requires you to be who you are." Brené Brown

The Masks We Wear

"I want freedom for the full expression of my personality." Mahatma Gandhi

Let's examine this for a moment. We now know our personality is made up of parts. The word personality is derived from the Latin word "mask." Simply put, our subpersonalities are the various masks we wear. Taking off our masks, moving in front of the masks, finding yourself in the mirror, is the work of returning to real. And that's what we are trying to do here - to befriend our parts - and reveal our soul's essence in its purest form. Compassionately getting to know our subpersonalities leads to the unmasking of our adaptive strategies and connects us to the core of our identity. You are no longer asleep to your unconscious beliefs and the masks your real self is hiding behind. You might remember the image at the beginning of the book where the Me part of you was small and overcome by all of your subpersonalities or what we describe as the We. The insights shared across the pages and the suggested REALignment practices have created the space to begin your journey to embracing all of your subpersonalities. As you can see in the image below the Me now holds within it, *all of you*. This is what we refer to as the We in Me.

Coming home to our real self sounds great, but it's often hard, messy, and monotonous. It is easier to stay hidden behind our masks and avoid the hard work of excavating our essence. After all, if you are going to unearth a treasure, your hands will get dirty. It is so important to walk this path with compassion. Awareness of what is can be painful and you may have experienced difficult moments throughout the book, as you engaged in the REALignment practices. We honour your commitment and congratulate you for sticking it out with us. Awareness is incredibly freeing. The good news is that with each REALignment practice, you are starting to create new neural pathways. As our subpersonalities soften, a deeper aspect of yourself emerges. This is the gift awaiting us.

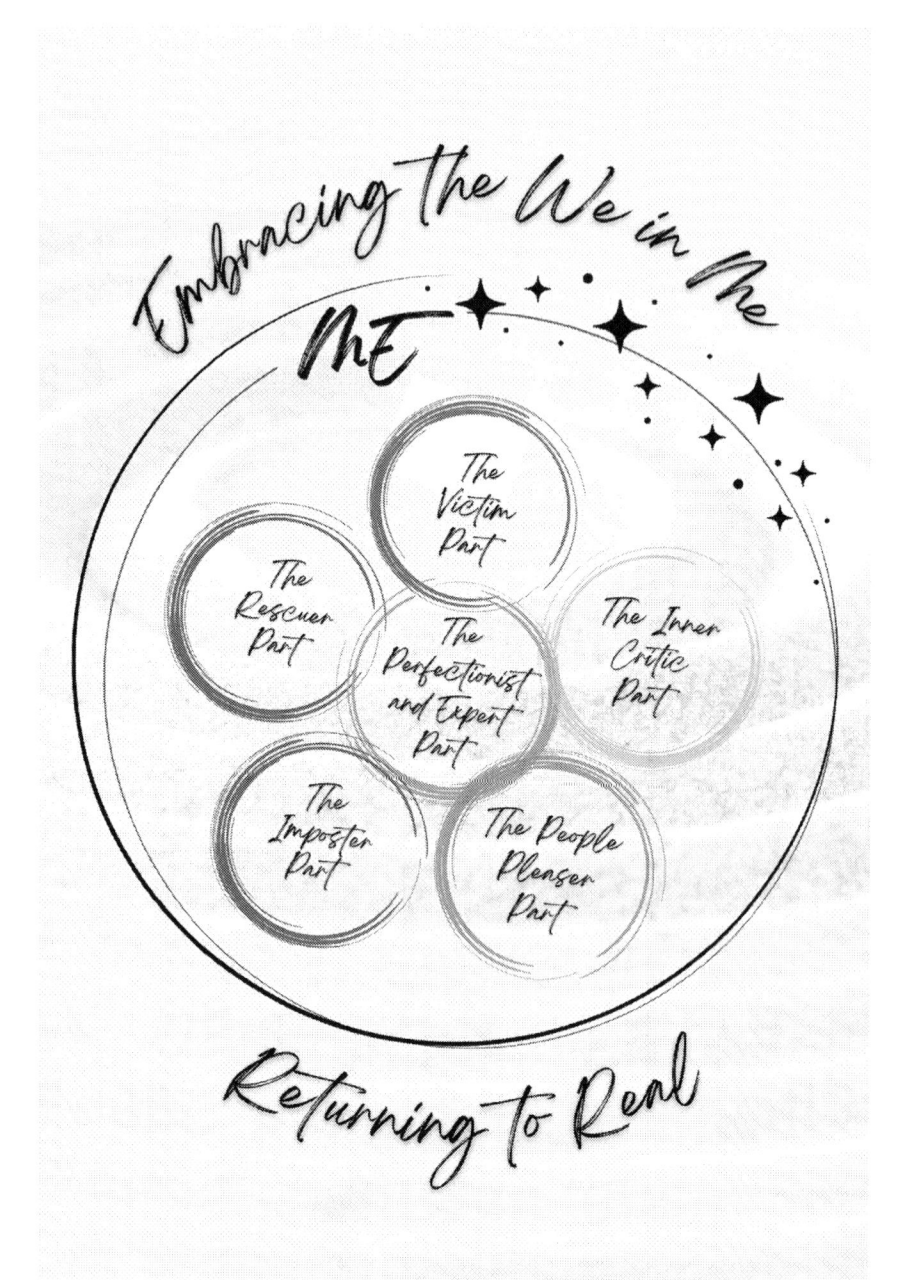

Embracing the We in Me

- The Victim Part
- The Rescuer Part
- The Inner Critic Part
- The Perfectionist and Expert Part
- The Imposter Part
- The People Pleaser Part

Returning to Real

What thoughts, longings, feelings, and beliefs come up for you when you think about finding your way home to your real self? Take a moment to reflect in this space.

_____
_____
_____
_____
_____
_____
_____
_____
_____
_____
_____
_____
_____

Getting to know our parts with compassion is a powerful tool for self-actualization. It liberates us to develop our true self by engaging in the practices necessary to access our inner wisdom. It also presents a bridge for understanding, with greater empathy, how our friends and loved ones walk through this world as well. Embody the consciousness of your subpersonalities, and you have a roadmap for wielding your powers inherent to your real self and the power of radical connectedness to yourself and others.

Integrate Instead of Compartmentalize

By befriending these seven subpersonalities you can live in harmony with them. This sets into motion a ripple effect of love and understanding that transforms not only your life, but the collective consciousness as well. Each practice carries the intention to manifest awareness. When you engage in these practices you are creating new neural pathways that change your brain. This expands your emotional capacity and increases flexibility to adapt. It expands your comfort zone and increases your emotional intelligence. You will notice more confidence and will find joy more often. You are no longer driven by a part; you can free yourself from the fixation of a part. Neuroscience and psychology tell us that self-led curiosity and compassion opens the door for love for yourself and others.

"Sometimes being real means allowing pain or accepting a painful truth. Yet something in us aligns with an inner ground of authenticity when we are real. We love it because of its inherent rightness in our soul, the sense of 'Aha, here I am, and there is nothing to do but be." A.H. Almaas

At the heart of this guidebook is the Raw, Risky & Real™ framework for creating life changes and living intentionally and deliberately. All of our parts reveal the interconnectedness of our experiences. In your purest essence, you know who you really are, your desired dreams and life's magic now lies within you. In order to heal and recover we must find internal validation.

Since you have gone through this guidebook, you now have an understanding that your parts' beliefs and values were developed out of necessity. We hope that you see the importance of loving all parts of yourself with empathy and compassion. Be careful not to be harsh, critical, or judgmental of any of your parts. Repeat the REALignment practices as many times as you need to. Being authentic is a daily choice. It's OK to be who you are even if some people want something else.

You Know the Rest

You will notice that, compared to the rest of the book, this is a short chapter. Very short. There's a reason for that; there is nothing else you need to hear from us. You don't need another chapter. This is where you take hold of the steering wheel and begin to drive your bus. Your journey begins. Your life through a new lens is waiting. You know what it takes to return to real and you know what you need to do.

So, let us ask you, how does the book end?

Let's imagine it ends like this:

....and then (insert your name) closed the book, took a few deep breaths and thought, "I *understand. Befriend and love the we in me, all of my parts.*" Start with the end in mind and put a foot on a path that will change your life forever. Simple daily disciplines, little productive actions, repeated consistently over time add up to the difference between being real and letting our subpersonalities take the lead.

You have looked at your parts, faced your past and yourself honestly and compassionately. You know that you cannot heal the things that you cannot feel. You have opened yourself to a new way of looking at yourself in the mirror. You are entering into a harmonious and loving relationship with the inner critic, the people pleaser, the expert, the imposter, the rescuer and the victim parts of yourself. On your journey you may encounter other parts of yourself that we haven't mentioned in this book, but we trust that you have the awareness and the recipe to enter into friendship with these parts of yourself. You are now in a position where you can begin releasing unrealistic expectations and can follow your own authentic values and passions. Our hearts are with you as you continue your lifelong path of discovery and recovery.

"If you want to be free, you must first accept that there is pain in your heart. You have stored it there. And You have done everything you can think of to keep it there, deep inside, so you never have to feel it. There is also tremendous joy, beauty, love and peace within you. But they are on the other side of the pain. On the other side of the pain is ecstasy. On the other side of freedom. Your true greatness lies on the other side of that layer of pain. You must be willing to accept pain in order to pass through to the other side. Just accept that it is in there and that you are going to feel it. Accept that if you relax, it will have its moment before your awareness, and then it will pass. It always does." Michael A. Singer

Life may seem linear, but it is a circle. Let us end where we began, with Raw, Risky & Real™.

RAW is about feeling our pain points. We all have painful raw wounds simply because we are humans living life. That is the human experience. RAW is the beginning and the birthplace of change.

R: RECOGNIZE all modes of information moving through you in body, mind, and spirit. Notice your thoughts, feelings, and body sensations. Do you feel expansive, alert, and expressive or tight, constricted, or short of breath? Bring awareness to the experience in your body. By acknowledging all that is present, we give ourselves permission to get curious. Focus on a particular space in your body that is calling for your attention. Stay with the sensation for as long as you can. As you stay with the sensation, think of a word that goes with it. If it could speak, what would it say? What does it need or want? Is there an emotion under this sensation?

A: ACKNOWLEDGE any discomfort or anything that is present in your body. Discomfort is a sign that you are triggered and that your past is showing up in your present. This is how you know a part has been activated.

W: WELCOME with compassion all that is present. This is the beginning of uncovering your parts, your subpersonalities.

To recap what you just read:

RECOGNIZE fully

ACKNOWLEDGE triggers

WELCOME parts

Subpersonalities have pure, honest intentions of protecting you from further pain and harm. As you get to know all parts of yourself, you will transform your relationship with difficult thoughts, feelings, and beliefs. We are creatures of habit, but we can change the way we dance with our subpersonalities by changing the music.

RISKY is about taking action.

"Courage is not the absence of fear, but fear walking." Susan David

Let's face it, it is risky to open up. This is where vulnerability dances with our adaptive strategies. We may fail, and that's OK. This is a journey and a circle that we will keep looping through.

This step is an incredible place for growth and change. This is where we will take action and engage in new practices. Creating new practices leads to manifesting new relationships with our subpersonalities and our real self.

Risky is an opportunity to reflect on your values and intentions so that you can write a new story. The story starts with being kind to ourselves and finding a balance that works for us.

R: REFLECTION: Reflecting on our values allows us to uncover what is meaningful and important to us from the perspective of our heart. Our values are the basic beliefs that determine our priorities and actions and they shape how we live, work and love. They measure whether or not our life is turning out the way we want to live. When our goals and choices align with our values, life is good. When our choices and goals do not align, we probably feel unhappy, stressed, or discontented with life. Your reflections provide clarity, direction, and motivate you to make important changes.

I: INTENTIONS: We provide ourselves accountability through intention setting, allowing us to take control of our choices and life. It's about being proactive in your own life, by purposely choosing how you want your life experience to be. Intentions prepare us for a moment in the future.

S: STORY: With intentions, we can write a new story for ourselves, filling the pages of the next chapter in our life. To truly change, we must first imagine what we want to create. Anything we can sense, feel, think about, observe, imagine can be manifested.

K: KINDNESS: Staring down our demons does not work. The push and pull of our parts' perceptions may attempt to sabotage our ability to write our new stories - our real life. We welcome each part with compassion and kindness.

Y: YEARNING: For any change to occur and to move us to the point of action we must want the change to occur. There must be a desire for something different.

To recap what you just read:

REFLECT on your values

Set INTENTIONS for what you want

Create the STORY of your life

Be KIND to all parts of yourself in the process

YEARN for what is possible

"You don't have to be great to start, but you have to start to be great." Zig Ziglar

REAL

We experience REAL as Brené Brown defines grounded confidence which is *"the messy process of learning and unlearning, practicing and failing, and surviving misses."*

Let's be clear, we don't arrive at REAL We continually practice it, learning and unlearning, failing and succeeding, surviving and thriving.

R: REALIZATION: That REAL part of you has and will always be with you. This isn't about finding or creating your authentic self because that part of you, let's call it your soul, is not lost or needing to be created. We speak of it as a return because it is the place we come from. It has simply been covered up by our coping mechanisms and subpersonalities. It gently and patiently awaits your return.

E: EXPANSION: We are continually growing, changing, and expanding. Returning to our deepest, truest selves involves a continuous expansion of self, shifting from a rigid mindset to a more flexible mindset which supports new ideas and thoughts about ourselves and our world.

A: ACCEPTANCE: Acceptance is the greatest pathway out of suffering. Acceptance does not mean we agree with the circumstances of our life; it does not mean we simply roll over and let what is occurring continue to happen. It means that we acknowledge that in this moment, this is our reality.

L: LOVE: Love is transcendental. It is formless. At our very core, we are pure love. Before we can see others through the eyes of love, we must first see ourselves in this light.

To recap what you just read:

REALIZE that your authentic self has always been with you

EXPAND in new ways

ACCEPT your reality

LOVE yourself

Thank you for taking our hand and walking this journey with us. From a place of love, we invite you to use this book as a living guide for your continued journey towards the REAL you.

ABOUT THE AUTHORS

Carmen Jelly Weiss, BA, MACP, RP

Carmen is a registered psychotherapist with more than 25 years experience in public and private practice. She is also a clinical supervisor and a certified practitioner of compassionate inquiry. She is the founder and director of her private practice, New Perceptions, working with clients and mentoring qualifying therapists on their certifying journey. She is a best-selling author in three previous books and creates podcasts sharing her growing body of knowledge in healing and personal development.

Please visit her website www.newperceptions.ca for information about psychotherapy, supervision, podcasts, workshops, and retreats.

ABOUT THE AUTHORS

Suzanne Rochon BSW, RSW

Suzanne is a Registered Social Worker with more than 25 years of experience in the public sector, with an equal amount of time in direct service and leadership roles. She is the founder of Imagine Life Solutions Counselling, working with a range of clients seeking to move from wounds to wellness. Trained in Compassionate Inquiry and with a background in Holistic Health Practices, she is able to blend a variety of approaches in her practice. She is the best-selling author of two collaborative books and enjoys creating podcasts to open the mind to new possibilities for growth and self-development.

Please visit her website www.imaginelifesolutions.ca for information about counselling, podcasts, workshops, and retreats.

REFERENCES

1wolfiesLady. (2010, February 13). *Elvis Presley- any way you want me (that's how I will be)*. YouTube. Retrieved August 5, 2020, from www.youtube.com/watch?v=nAL3IOV0kF0

50 Robin Sharma quotes to inspire and motivate you - the inspiring journal. (n.d.). Retrieved May 6, 2020, from www.theinspiringjournal.com/50-robin-sharma-quotes/

A&E Networks Television. (2022, September 15). *Dalai Lama*. Biography.com. Retrieved November 30, 2021, from www.biography.com/religious-figure/dalai-lama

Alder, S. L. (2018). *The narcissistic abuse recovery bible: Spiritual recovery from narcissistic and emotional abuse.* CFI, an imprint of Cedar Fort, Inc.

Alice Miller - child abuse and mistreatment. Alice Miller en | Child abuse. (n.d.). Retrieved April 4, 2020, from www.alice-miller.com/en/

Alice quotes. The 76 Best Alice Quotes. (n.d.). Retrieved November 5, 2022, from bookroo.com/quotes/alice

Alice X. Huang, MD, MS. (2021). Retrieved June 2, 2021, from alicehuangmd.com/

Almaas, A. H. (1997). *Diamond Heart* ;A. H. Almaas.

Almaas | Ridhwan. (n.d.). Retrieved February 21, 2020, from www.diamondapproach.org/almaas

Almaas, A. (2000). *The freedom to be*. Penguin Random House.

Anne Wilson Schaef. Living in Process. (2020, March 6). Retrieved June 5, 2020, from livinginprocess.com/anne-wilson-schaef/

Arkin, R. M. (n.d.). *Self-concept and self-presentation*.

Beattie, M. (2009). *The language of Letting go*. Phoenix Audio.

Beattie, M., & Beattie, M. (1992). *Codependent no more; &, beyond codependency*. MJF Books.

Brach, T. (2020). *Radical compassion: Learning to love yourself and your world with the practice of rain*. Rider Books.

Brach, T., & Kornfield, J. (2004). *Radical acceptance: Embracing your life with the heart of a buddha*. Bantam Books.

REFERENCES

Brown, B. (2012). *Daring greatly: How the courage to be vulnerable transforms the way we live, Love, parent, and lead.* Baker & Taylor.

Brown Brene'. (2017). *Rising strong how the ability to reset transforms the way we live, Love, parent, and lead.* Random House Inc.

Brown Brene'. (2019). *Braving the wilderness: The quest for true belonging and the courage to stand alone.* Random House.

Brown, B. (2020). *The gifts of imperfection.* Random House.

Brown, B. (2022). *Atlas of the heart.* Random House.

Cohen, Alan. (n.d.). Retrieved October 4, 2020, from *Programs & Publications* www.alancohen.com/

Cohen, A. (2015). *A course in miracles made easy: Mastering the journey from Fear to love.* Hay House, Inc.

Courses. Dr. Gabor Maté. (2020, May 10). Retrieved November 5, 2022, from drgabormate.com/courses/

David, S. (2018). *Emotional agility.* Penguin USA.

David, S. (n.d.). *Susan David.* TED. Retrieved March 20, 2021-, from www.ted.com/speakers/susan_david

Dyer, D. W. (1978). *Pulling your own strings.* Hamlyn.

Finn, A. (2022, May 27). *100 pink quotes to make your day lovely and sweet.* Quote Ambition. Retrieved November 5,

2022, from www.quoteambition.com/pink-quotes/

Gaille, B. (2017, January 13). *28 stupendous Rick Hanson quotes*. BrandonGaille.com. Retrieved March 27, 2022, from brandongaille.com/28-stupendous-rick-hanson-quotes

Goalcast. (2022, August 21). *Top 35 most famous and inspiring Mahatma Gandhi quotes*. Goalcast. Retrieved November 19, 2021, from www.goalcast.com/top-20-inspiring-mahatma-gandhi-quotes/

Goodreads. (n.d.). *A quote by Peggy O'Mara*. Goodreads. Retrieved October 13, 2021, from www.goodreads.com/quotes/597503-the-way-we-talk-to-our-children-becomes-their-inner

Goodreads. (n.d.). *Alan Cohen quotes (author of a course in miracles made easy)*. Goodreads. Retrieved January 17, 2021, from www.goodreads.com/author/quotes/19734.Alan_Cohen

Goodreads. (n.d.). *Anne Hathaway quotes (author of the Homecraft book)*. Goodreads. Retrieved February 21, 2021, from www.goodreads.com/author/quotes/53794.Anne_Hathaway

Goodreads. (n.d.). *Anne Wilson Schaef quotes (author of meditations for women who do too much)*. Goodreads. Retrieved November 5, 2022, from

REFERENCES 151

www.goodreads.com/author/quotes/160417.Anne_Wilson_Schaef

Goodreads. (n.d.). *Peggy O'Mara (author of Natural Family Living)*. Goodreads. Retrieved November 5, 2022, from www.goodreads.com/author/show/30657.Peggy_O_Mara

Goodreads. (n.d.). *Susan David Quotes (author of emotional agility)*. Goodreads. Retrieved November 5, 2022, from www.goodreads.com/author/quotes/7118701.Susan_David

Goodreads. (n.d.). *Zig Ziglar quotes (author of see you at the top)*. Goodreads. Retrieved December 3, 2022, from www.goodreads.com/author/quotes/50316.Zig_Ziglar

Hanson, R. (2016). *Hardwiring Happiness: The New Brain Science of contentment, calm, and confidence.* Harmony Books.

Hanson, R. (2018). *Resilient.* Random House.

Kubler-Ross Elizabeth. (1972). *On death and dying.* Yomiuri shinbunsha.

Lancer Darlene. (2022). *Codependency for dummies.* John Wiley & Sons.

Maraboli, S. (2013). *Unapologetically you: Reflections on life and the human experience.* A Better Today.

Maraboli, S. (2014). *Life, the truth, & being free.* A Better Today.

Mate', Gabor. (2018). *In the realm of hungry ghosts.* Vermillion.

Maté, Gabor. (1999). *Scattered: How attention deficit disorder originates and what you can do about it.* Dutton.

Maté, Gabor. (2019). *When the body says no: The cost of Hidden Stress.* Ebury Digital.

McConnell, S. (2020). *Somatic Internal Family Systems therapy: Awareness, breath, resonance, movement, and touch in practice.* North Atlantic Books.

Media, I. R. B. (2021). *Summary of Kristen Neff's self-compassion.* IRB Media.

Miller, A. (1996). *Prisoners of childhood: The drama of The gifted child and the search for the true self.* Basic Books a division of HarperCollins Publishers.

Mooney, C. G. (2010). *Theories of attachment an introduction to Bowlby, Ainsworth, Gerber, Brazelton, Kennell, and Klaus.* Redleaf Press.

Neff, Kristen. *Self-compassion.* Self. (2022, October 11). Retrieved December 10, 2021, from self-compassion.org/about-kristin-neff/

Obama, M. (2021). *Becoming.* Crown.

Oprah.com. (n.d.). Retrieved September 20, 2020, from www.oprah.com/index.html

Pincott, J. (2014, February 5). *How to outsmart your ego.* Oprah.com. Retrieved September 9, 2021, from www.oprah.com/spirit/tame-your-ego-research-on-ego/all

S.k., & S.r. (n.d.). *Centre for Love and compassion.* Maitri Centre. Retrieved February 13, 2021, from www.selfcompassion.ca/

# REFERENCES

Salzberg, S. (2018). *Real love: The art of mindful connection*. Flatiron Books.

Sri Sri Ravi Shankar, Gurudev. (2022, August 23). *Humanitarian and spiritual leader* Retrieved January 26, 2022, from www.srisriravishankar.org/

Remen, R. N. (1994). *Wounded healers*. Wounded Healer Press.

Schwartz, Richard. (2020). *Introduction to Internal Family Systems*. Sounds True.

Schwartz, Richard. (2021). *No bad parts*. Sounds True.

Sharma, Robin. *Official Website of the #1 Bestselling Author*. (n.d.). Retrieved December 30, 2021, from www.robinsharma.com/

Sharma, R. (2020). *The 5AM club*. HarperCollins UK.

Singer, M. A. (2013). *The untethered soul: The journey beyond yourself*. Noetic Books, Institute of Noetic Sciences, New Harbinger Publications, Inc.

Team, G. T. E. (2018, December 2). *Internal Family Systems (IFS)*. Internal Family Systems Therapy. Retrieved May 2, 2021, from www.goodtherapy.org/learn-about-therapy/types/internal-family-systems-therapy

Tolle, E. (2005). *The power of now: A guide to spiritual enlightenment*. Hodder Mobius.

Top 25 quotes by Henri Nouwen (of 497): A-Z quotes. A. (n.d.). Retrieved November 5, 2022, from www.azquotes.com/author/10905-Henri_Nouwen

Top 25 quotes by Brené Brown (of 321): A-Z quotes. A. (n.d.). Retrieved November 1, 2020, from www.azquotes.com/author/19318-Brene_Brown

Top 25 quotes by Henri Nouwen (of 497): A-Z quotes. A. (n.d.). Retrieved November 5, 2022, from www.brainyquote.com/authors/henri-nouwen-quotes

Top 25 quotes by Maya Angelou (of 1010): A-Z quotes. A. (n.d.). Retrieved November 5, 2022, from www.azquotes.com/author/440-Maya_Angelou

Wang, K. (2021). *Imposter syndrome.* Booktopia editions.

Wayne Dyer - the official website of dr. Wayne W. Dyer. Dr. Wayne W. Dyer. (2015, September 9). Retrieved April 15, 2021, from www.drwaynedyer.com/

Western, D. (2022, July 20). 55 *most inspiring Madonna quotes.* Wealthy Gorilla. Retrieved June 21, 2021, from wealthygorilla.com/55-inspiring-madonna-quotes/

Wikimedia Foundation. (2022, October 3). *Henri Nouwen.* Wikipedia. Retrieved April 14, 2021, from www.en.wikipedia.org/wiki/Henri_Nouwen

Williamson, M. (2015). *A return to love: Reflections on the principles of a course in miracles.* Amazon. Retrieved November 1, 2021, from www.amazon.com/Return-Love-Reflections-Principles-Miracles/dp/0060927488

Williams, K. J. (1987). *Victim mentality: Victims of family violence as caregivers to the abusers.*

Xplore. (n.d.). *Henri Nouwen quotes*. Brainy Quote. Retrieved November 11, 2021, from www.brainyquote.com/authors/henri-nouwen-quotes

Xplore. (n.d.). *Lady Gaga quotes*. Brainy Quote. Retrieved November 5, 2022, from www.brainyquote.com/authors/lady-gaga-quotes

Xplore. (n.d.). *Lao Tzu quotes*. Brainy Quote. Retrieved March 16, 2021, from www.brainyquote.com/authors/lao-tzu-quotes

Zukav, G. (2014). *The seat of the soul: 25th anniversary edition*. Simon & Schuster.

Manufactured by Amazon.ca
Bolton, ON